Forbidden Texts

Forbidden Texts

*Erotic Literature and its Readers
in Eighteenth-Century France*

JEAN MARIE GOULEMOT

Translated by James Simpson

UNIVERSITY OF PENNSYLVANIA PRESS
Philadelphia

This English translation © Polity Press 1994.
First published in France as *Ces livres qu'on ne lit que d'une main* © 1991
Editions Alinea.

First published in 1994 by Polity Press in association with Blackwell
Publishers.

First published in the United States in 1994 by the University of Pennsylvania Press.

Published with the assistance of the French Ministry of Culture.

ISBN 0-8122-3319-0

Typeset in 11 on 13 pt Sabon
by Graphicraft Typesetters Ltd., Hong Kong
Printed in Great Britain by T.J. Press, Padstow, Cornwall

This book is printed on acid-free paper.

U.S. Library of Congress Card Catalog No. 94-12045

Contents

List of Illustrations

Preface

This brief essay is not intended as a comprehensive history of erotic or pornographic literature in the eighteenth century, even though the sheer quantity of material and its importance, all too well attested, would amply justify such an enterprise.[1] Thus what we have is neither a catalogue, an *Enfer* for dix-huitiémistes, nor a list of recommended authors (or even unrecommendable ones, depending on your point of view), nor a list of seizures, nor even a survey of themes or narrative sequences typical of the genre (which in itself would rapidly become boring).[2] Since the description of sexual activity in these works is made up of repeated sequences and stock figures, pornography quickly grows boring. Nobody can fail to be aware of this fact, whether they have only an inkling of it, or whether they have experienced it for themselves. What I intend to do is something quite different: to reflect on what it is to read pornographic literature, based on examples taken from the most salacious literature the eighteenth century has to offer. This reflection does not look at the motivation for reading such literature, or the forms it takes and the way in which these are then socially determined (Why did people read it? Where did they read it? In what form did they read it? Did they read it in private in the antechamber or in a boudoir in the company of others? Or did they read it alone in a silent yet crowded daydream?), but rather on the position of the reader as dictated by the writerly practices of the text itself.

In order to draw together and to understand the effect that

pornographic literature both produces and seeks to produce, whether it is accepted or not, we will centre our examination around the notion of the pornographic speech-act (*énonciation pornographique*). Reading pornographic literature is born out of a desire which is not simply the desire to read. Although that desire is reinforced by the very act of reading (how, though?), it cannot be satisfied. Erotic works lay bare the effects of reading, and of that intention that the writing of fiction bears in itself, to produce imaginary objects that present themselves and act as if they were real. Without wishing to be excessively provocative, what I will present here is the analysis of the pornographic novel as the novel itself stripped bare (if you will pardon the pun), right down to its very blueprint. For does not the erotic novel succeed, rather better than its more mainstream and more respectable brother narratives, in having the reader take illusion for reality and the word for the object? To all those who would dispute such a fact, we might cite as evidence the physical effects that it provokes,[3] the psychological troubles that it brings and the many prohibitions applied to it. In that respect it is far more effective than the *roman sentimental*, which, although it might well have had some effect on the men of the eighteenth century, does not often reduce its readers to tears in our own time.

We nonetheless know that readers of *La Nouvelle Héloïse* shed bitter tears over the death of Julie[4] and that racking sobs were inevitably the accompaniment as Bernadin de Saint-Pierre's Virginie met her watery end. However, the fact that both men and women at this period were easily moved to tears (did not the eighteenth century invent the 'tear-jerker', the *drame larmoyant*, after all?) is not really an explanation. The fact that Diderot weeps at the return of his friend Grimm, after a week's absence, is proof of a readiness to be moved to tears that is rather out of fashion.[5] And yet the fact that people needed to have an excuse to cry does not mean that they did not exercise some choice over the right moment. The audience of *Le Mariage de Figaro* were not touched to the same degree on hearing of the unhappy marriage of the virtuous countess, abandoned in spite of her fidelity. A range of emotional conditioning, a certain theatricization of sentiment and a certain narrative strategy in the novel, a certain approach to story-telling and to moving the audience, all played their part. Some succeeded in this, and some failed. To take an example, the erotic writing of the eighteenth century presents us with just such a paradox. The violence depicted in the works of Sade – the misfortunes that afflict Justine, the attacks on Madame de Mistival in *La Philosophie dans le boudoir*, as well as the tortures inflicted on the prisoners in the *Cent-vingt journées de Sodome* – far from eliciting compassion and tears, were supposed to delight its readers and give rise to sexual excitement. The sight of tears does not necessarily give rise to tears in return. In this century that was supposed to be so virtuous, the suffering and misery of another human being were not always an invitation to compassion as much as they were an incitement to pleasure and *jouissance*.

As much as to say that it would be far too simple to reduce the eighteenth century to a sensibility easily moved to tears, or to a superficial sensuality. The reader weeps or feels desire as a result of particular devices deployed at a narrative or descriptive level. On the one hand, there are tears and sentimentality, and on the other, obscenity and the intent to arouse. However, if Diderot weeps in causing the death of his heroine, Suzanne Simonin, in *La Religieuse*, and if a given reader of the *Portier des Chartreux* illustrates, by the emotion felt, an affirmation of Jean-Jacques Rousseau according to which there are books that one can only read with one hand,[6] we also know that modern readers no longer weep at the misfortunes that befall Julie and Saint-Preux. These tearful reactions are the product of a particular period: the melodrama that drew tears from our grandmothers often makes us laugh out loud. It should nonetheless be recognized that the *Portier des Chartreux*[7] still appears in collections of pornographic writing as if pornography in some way transcended history and changes in taste. The erotic effect survives the passage of time and seems to offer little grounding to a history of love that reveals more or less depending on time, place or individual personality.

We know that a number of pornographic books are simply older works hastily pressed into service. We take the same ones and begin again, changing names, decor and language. Like Etienne

Souriau, who listed the 200,000 possible dramatic situations,[8] one might well be tempted to make a list of all possible erotic situations. This would not be a simple listing of sexual positions with their possible permutations, but rather more the way they are set into the narrative, and thus their construction as pieces of writing. Without undertaking such a task, what ought to be within the bounds of possibility would be a relatively limited repertory of narrative situations found in pornographic works, with their sequential organization, containing virtually all the devices found in the novels that exist at present or that remain to be written.

By means of the accounts left by the historians in the *Cent-vingt journées de Sodome*, Sade offers a systematic working-through of all sexual perversions. As one might guess, the story is cut short: what can happen after the murder of the partners? How can one transcend that and write of what is intended to be the ultimate *jouissance*? Sade's manuscript ends with a list of victims, their names savagely crossed out, as if to prove the existence of something that was unsayable. Pleasure, where is your dominion? Writing, here is the moment of your defeat! However, should one deduce from this that pornography has no history other than that of its external features in Western societies? Although the hypothesis is plausible, we will not seek to confirm it. Rather the object of this study is literature itself, and quite specifically its function in the reading process. Pornography would be only a test case in this regard, but all the more well suited to illustrate how we read fictional texts.

As much as to say that our analysis will bear on more than simply the flesh and blood reader, in terms of his reality as a man of his time and in terms of his cultural habits, and actually on the erotic text itself, since we postulate that the pornographic book conditions the reader, and indeed constitutes its reading to the point that one takes that which is imaginary for the truth, with all the physical consequences that might be expected to result from such a confusion.

What we have then is a text and its contexts: that is to say, a form of writing deploying devices and narrative structures to appeal to the reader, consulted furtively before being bought or borrowed, often with a false air of detachment, but not without a certain feverishness. Because it is forbidden, such a text must designate itself as fast as possible, announce what it promises and allow some hint of its potential so as to guarantee its effects. Last of all, the work must put the reader in a position to experience its erotic effects. One might add to that the strategy of accompaniment and doubling that is put into operation through illustrations, the design of the page and the play of intertextual references. We must therefore speak of the erotic book as a material, cultural and literary object, whose goal is to force the reader into a desiring quest. This is no small task. We can therefore offer only a small sketch, limited in time: for the most part, the books referred to will be from the eighteenth century, and limited to the few that we are foolish enough to believe are representative of the strategies deployed by that work, most common and yet most rare: the erotic book.

Introduction:
'Les mots et les choses'

We begin with a few definitions, the words used then and now, with their differences and evolutions, disappearances and transformations. This is an elementary task, but less simple than it might appear, for the vocabulary of love is constantly expanding.[1] Each couple invents the lexis of their bodies and what they do by imposing shifts in meaning, or by specific transfers and new coinages. The expression 'faire cattleya' found in *A la recherche du temps perdu* is only one example of a widespread and yet profoundly private practice.[2] It is common in salacious texts, jokes and adolescent games that any word can be charged with erotic significance. Nothing can remain innocent or neutral. There is a systematic attempt to destabilize all the apparent specialization of vocabulary. This is perhaps even the basis of all prurience: to find hidden meanings, to play on ambiguities and to invent competing meanings without any rhyme or reason. Certain texts make use of and even abuse this principle, a well-known example being Diderot's *Les Bijoux indiscrets*; a less well-known one might be Sylvain Maréchal's *L'Araignée*, published in the collection *Contes saugrenus*.[3] The principle lies less in plays on extant double meanings than of attributing erotic meanings to any word by means of a process of contamination, once the decision has been made to enter that register. On the other hand, what we will not be dealing with is the sort of paranoiac interpretation as exemplified by Salvador Dali's obsessional reading of Millet's *Angelus*.[4] The diagnosis would be altogether too crude. Rather, all we wish to do here is to recall the process of eroticization that can often operate on a language that is not of itself immediately associated with love.

Our intention in this chapter is to deal with the public domain and the vocabulary that was used in the eighteenth century to designate the texts and images that we would call pornographic, obscene or smutty. This treatment will play on a certain anachronism by way of a late tribute to the sellers of suggestive postcards and the private cinemas that lined the boulevard de Clichy in my adolescent years.

The term *pornographique* is not used in eighteenth-century France. In 1769, Rétif de la Bretonne published *Le Pornographe* ('The Pornographer'),[5] but this was a treatise putting forward proposals for the regulation of prostitution in order to make of it a social practice rationalized in accordance with the principles of the Enlightenment. As history has taught us rather cruelly, the languages of reform and of womanizing make rather poor bedfellows. Official language is serious and even rather schoolmasterish, at any rate always moralistic; it avoids equivocation and anything that might give the lie to the serious image it wishes to present of itself. The impulse to regulate, so much a part of the militant atmosphere of the end of the Enlightenment, never goes astray in the uncertain paths of amorous innuendo. At the opposite end of the spectrum, even though it does not yet figure in any of the first editions of the dictionaries published by the Académie, either by Furetière or Richelet, the term *érotique* is currently and widely used during the period. The *Encyclopédie* compiled by Diderot and d'Alembert defines the word as referring to the anacreontic ode (that is to say, odes in the style of the poet Anacreon), which takes 'amour et galanterie' as its subject matter. The work underlines the fact that the word belongs to the domain of medical pathology: 'everything that pertains to love between the sexes; the term is used particularly to characterize the delirium caused by dissolute living, and excessive bodily appetites in this regard, which causes the individual to look upon the object of that passion as the sovereign good, and causes him to wish for ardent union. It is a form of melancholic affectation, a true illness . . .'. But make no mistake: if we believe the dictionaries, then erotic love (the word *érotisme* is not used) is not to be confused with either the female condition of *fureur utérine* ('furor uterinus' or 'nymphomania') or the male condition of satyriasis, 'because it gives way to pudor and to finer feeling'. To judge from the texts of the eighteenth century, one might well get the impression that what is meant by *érotique* is all that which pertains to the matter of love, which makes the word subject to all sorts of extensions of usage and a great deal of imprecision.

However, at the same time, the terms that are used to designate texts and images whose goal is to produce sexual excitation are now completely outdated: *licencieux* ('licentious'), *obscène* ('obscene'), the latter being still in use, but also used for objects and behaviours that have nothing to do with sensuality, *lascif* ('lascivious') and, last of all, *lubrique* ('lubricious'). These words form a group but are not all part of the same perspective. *Licencieux* and *obscène* imply a moral judgement. The *Encyclopédie* notes that *obscène* 'describes that which is contrary to pudor. An obscene speech, painting or book.' And, by way of example, the *Encyclopédie* offers that following: 'obscenity in conversation is the resort of the ignorant, fools and libertines. There are such ill-formed minds that see obscenity in all things.' Furetière's dictionary gives the following entry for the term *licencieux*: 'he who takes too much freedom and licence. This young man is too licentious in speech: he says things that are far too bold or foul or impious. He lives the licentious life of a libertine.' We see that *licencieux* also alludes to *libertinage* of mind as well as of habits, and can therefore see the confusion on which the general denunciation of libertines reposed. As for the term *lascif*, Furetière insists more on the effects produced: 'Somebody given to, or that which leads to luxuriousness and incontinence. Pictures, postures, books, words, and all that which might excite one to unseemly or dishonest actions or thoughts. He-goats are stinking and lascivious.' If one is speaking from a religious point of view, then the term used is *concupiscence* ('covetousness'): 'Covetousness [is defined as] unregulated passion to possess something. It is forbidden by the tenth commandment of God's law that one should covet one's neighbours goods . . . It is used more particularly of the passions that tend towards dishonest love, that Paul terms the covetousness of the eyes or of the flesh.' We might add to the list to give it yet more weight the terms paillard ('lewd'), libre ('broad', 'free' or 'loose'), galant ('gallant') and also lubrique, the antonym of pudique, which corresponds to obscène in a cause–effect relationship. Only the point of view changes. Either one observes the object that provokes (which is then obscène or lubrique) or one examines the effects produced on the spectator (and the term then used is lascif). According to the Encyclopédie, lubricité is 'a term that designates an excessive leaning for women on the part of the man, or for men on the part of the woman, when this is demonstrated by external actions contrary to decency . . . It points to a violent temperament: it promises a great deal of pleasure and little restraint in sexual pleasure . . . Shamelessness ['impudicité'] would then be an acquired vice, and lubriciousness a natural fault.'

From this survey of the lexical material to be found in the most commonly used dictionaries of the eighteenth century, there are two major points to be retained. First of all, the multiple points of view that are put into operation in order to perceive and evaluate (either positively or negatively) a state of sexual excitation, and then the place accorded in these definitions to the other, a seduced and captive partner. It is not for nothing that St Paul, if one is to believe Furetière's *Dictionnaire universel*, speaks of the covetousness of the eyes and the flesh. The terms *obscène* and *lascif* convey an awareness of the theatricization of seduction. There is a presence and a presentation of the body as sexual, but also the presence of the gaze that perceives, scrutinizes and is troubled. The literature of the time has already fully mapped these possibilities and oppositions.

It now remains for us to explore the language of artists, and more especially of those whose task it is to recognize and denounce those works that represent a threat to accepted standards of behaviour and morals: men of the law or of the Church, magistrates and priests. We shall give particular attention to the

Mémoires sur la librairie et sur la liberté de presse, composed by Lamoignon de Malesherbes in 1759 and published in 1814.[6] Malesherbes divides into four categories those books 'that might be truly reprehensible'. 'Some', he notes, 'interest individuals, others are of interest to the government, and others are for the attention of the Church and those concerned with morality.' Hence the four headings: personal satires, books against the government, books that are contrary to accepted standards of decency, and lastly books that are anti-religious or atheistic in content. It is the third heading that interests us most here: Malesherbes distinguishes between licentious and obscene literature. 'Those works generally said to be contrary to accepted standards of decency are those which are obscene or simply licentious. Obscenity must be forbidden. All laws agree on this point, and everyone is of one mind, and the laws that are given to censors can be easily observed.' The difference between the obscene and the licentious, according to Malesherbes, is simply a question of degree: between that which must be repressed and that which can be tolerated. 'As regards those books that are merely licentious, such as La Fontaine's *Contes*, or Rousseau's *Epigrammes* ... it would be better that they were simply repressed, but the question remains as to what would give us a clear guideline in this respect? Some good people, whom I think too rigorous, would go so far as to forbid anything that they thought too likely to inspire any tenderness of feeling. I do not think that there is any state official who deems such severity necessary.' Implying that since the control of literary production was impossible, and that since licentiousness was not dangerous in itself, and that the application of such restrictive legislation was impossible, the best thing seemed to be to opt for a rather more tolerant approach. Another tone altogether is adopted for obscenity: 'Obscenity can be completely eradicated, or at least be very much restricted, since it is possible to assign to it the most serious penalties. However, the relaxed nature of current standards does not allow us to make similar pronouncements against broad ['libres'] or licentious works ...'

The distinctions and measures proposed by Malesherbes allow us to understand how, for the statesman looking for effective measures, lexical subtleties are scarcely appropriate. The criteria adopted were dictated by practical considerations. Would it be possible or not to impose the measures? Were the works targeted genuinely harmful? Would these two criteria allow for a reduction of what was rather a broad lexical field to two large categories that reflected not only a hierarchy of that which was tolerable, but also a sweep of opinion on the dangers of reading?

We know that the Church did not stop pursuing what it termed 'mauvais livres' ('evil works') at any point in the century: condemnations, pastoral letters and warnings to the public were all used. Some denunciations have become notorious: Helvétius' *De l'esprit*, the condemnation of *Emile* by Christophe de Beaumont, Archbishop of Paris, or those of Voltaire's *Dictionnaire philosophique* and Holbach's *Système de la nature*.[7] However, these isolated *causes célèbres* do tend nonetheless to make the reader forget the sheer scale of the war against those books that were deemed to be anti-religious or simply immoral under the broad heading of 'effets d'incredulité', the harm that they would do in spreading unbelief. Of course, the Church's onslaught cannot be reduced to a simple clash with the Enlightenment: what was at stake was something wider still. The Church presented itself not only as the guardian of religious orthodoxy but also of morals, and any book that it judged 'capable of affecting purity of faith or promoting moral corruption' (*Instruction pastorale de Monseigneur l'Illustrissime et révérendissime évêque d'Arras et Avertissement du clergé de France sur les funestes effets de l'incrédulité*, Arras, 1770) was dangerous or suspect. We might include under the same heading those 'impious and licentious books', that, according to the Bishop of Châlons (*Lettre pastorale contre la lecture des mauvais livres*, 1769), 'spill out from the capital and flow on into the provinces, where they destroy religion and morals.' It is not rare that condemnation is reserved almost exclusively for those licentious works that 'appeal to the imagination of our corrupted youth and sow impurity along with sexual desire.' In the same movement the Church also attacks 'the Atheist . . ., the Materialist . . ., the Epicurean . . ., the Libertine' (*Avertissement du clergé de France*, 1770), and takes care to show the strategy lying behind materialist apology for the pleasures of the flesh. Impiety and impurity are both targeted. 'Moral corruption is indeed a violent temptation against the faith!' Pornographic literature and materialist philosophy share the same corrupting effects, for the same weapon serves the same end, and that weapon was seduction. The seduction of the senses by the illusions of pornographic writing was assimilated to the seductions of philosophy. The good Christian needed to be armed against both in advance, and what was at stake was nothing less than his soul.

Such reactions give us some idea of how the clerical notion of the erotic novel could be extended to include a number of other works. This stems from the perspective adopted by the episcopal letters and condemnations issued. The problem is less the means that were deployed to seduce (as the Evil One seduces) than the goal they had in mind: the corruption of souls and eternal damnation. This did not mean that the anathemas pronounced against such works did not revel in the details of their analyses of the effects produced by licentious literature: 'An unreflecting youth gives itself up ardently to seductive readings, soon to find there the wrack of its faith and its virtue, soon to learn how to shake off the yoke of a religion whose austere morality weighs heavy on a heart so tossed by passions as it is at that age . . .'

It would not be entirely out of place to recall the rather more nuanced position held by Massillon, a well-known preacher from the end of the reign of Louis XIV and the beginning of the regency. A member of the Académie, Bishop of Clermont, a man admired by Voltaire for his style, he did not share the worries of other churchmen over the social and political threat posed by the reading of such wicked books. In his *Discours inédit sur le danger des mauvaises lectures* published in 1817, almost certainly written in his retreat in Clermont, he distinguishes frivolous and lascivious books without being too much preoccupied by works that were dangerous from a religious or political point of view. 'There are, I believe', he wrote, 'two kinds of dangerous books: those that are frivolous and those that are lascivious. The former lead to a dissipation of the mind and weaken us in the pursuit of grace, leaving us apt to forget God, while the latter corrupt the

heart and lead man into unbelief' (p. 1). However, those frivolous works which seem to be relatively neutral and not to represent any moral or spiritual danger as such are not entirely innocent.
'These works', Massillon notes, 'while they attack neither morality nor religion, and while they do not attack the words of the
Gospels or the teachings of Our Lord Jesus Christ, nonetheless
contain nothing but foolishness and the sort of senseless trifles
that are not worth a moment of the free time of a Christian . . .'
(p. 2). The reading of frivolous works impinges on meditation
and prayer and the exercise of charity: 'While your mind is absorbed in the reading of these idle works, the poor are knocking
at your door to ask for a crust of bread to ease their hunger and
you refuse it to them . . .' (p. 3). Massillon's position is not far
from that of Pascal: the book whose content is so trifling incites
its reader to sin because it is a diversion from meditation and
charity. ' . . . Instead of using up your days and nights in childish
amusements, why do you not rather devote them to taming your
lusts, in the mortification of your senses, and in the sacrifice of
your flesh so that it may not revolt and turn against you . . .' Such
a position is hostile to secular learning, of course, deeming salvation more urgent. Harmful in so far as they distract from what
is essential, a trifling book is nonetheless not dangerous for its
content, unlike the lascivious work, whose perverse effect is immediate. 'It is there that crime passes for weakness, the law of
marriage for an irrelevant scruple, and pudor for prejudice; it is
there that the wife learns to deceive her husband's eye, to violate
the sanctity of the marital bed that even the Heathen respect' (p.
8). Thus the lesser effect is simply the thin end of the wedge: the
reader of such works proceeds from faults of omission and neglect
to sins willingly committed. What this means is that the lascivious, as we have said, has the power not merely to fascinate, but
also to induce to act. Between those books that are said to be
trifling and those that are said to be lascivious there is the difference between passivity and activity.

It is clear from this analysis that the words used to designate
the licentious novel constitute a coherent and fairly homogenous
whole. Everything depends on the point of view adopted and the

institution involved. Malesherbes does not adopt the same norms as the bishops writing their pastoral letters. The defence of morality is not be confused with defence of the faith, even though the Church might have done so. The records of arrest and imprisonment at the Bastille carry the laconic quality of administrative language to its extreme point: people were interned for having published or hawked books that were either forbidden or prohibited or contrary to religion or accepted standards. Nothing is said, and yet everything is quite clear.

In the present text we have used the words 'pornographic', 'erotic' and 'licentious' as synonyms. This conflation will perhaps clash with contemporary values and semantic distinctions; however, such a range of synonyms will make the writing of this history easier and has the additional value of reflecting some of the realities of French usage in the eighteenth century.

1

The Importance of Erotic Literature in the Eighteenth Century

LOOKING BACK

Even if you had no access to specialist bibliographies such as that compiled by Guillaume Apollinaire, Ferdinand Fleuret and Louis Perceau: *L'Enfer de la Bibliothèque nationale* (Paris, 1911), or Pascal Pia's *Les Livres de L'Enfer, du XVIe siècle à nos jours* (Paris, 1978), it would still be possible to measure the vogue for erotic literature in the eighteenth century. All you would have to do would be to read the incessant condemnations issued by religious authorities and the measures taken by the police against those caught hawking works thought to be 'contrary to accepted moral standards'. These facts provide proof of its growing success that is further confirmed by Enlightenment tastes for a salaciousness that could serve its militant ends. Can we entirely ignore certain pages of *L'Ingénu* or of *La Religieuse*, certain colourful and suggestive scenes from *Jacques le Fataliste*, or the highly suggestive little fable *Les Bijoux indiscrets*, or the questionable charm of *Le Temple de Gnide*? From the very moment of Louis XIV's death and the accession of his regent, proof of the new importance literature accorded to the pleasures of the body is all too plain to see.

Not that the seventeenth century was entirely devoid of erotic literature. One need only recall the apparently insatiable demand for translations of the works of Pietro Aretino[1] (known to the French simply as 'L'Arétin'), and that some of the more marginal, more free-booting poets were quite happy to make abundant sacrifice at the altar of Venus. In a pretence of classical learning, well-schooled libertines sometimes penned erotic or obscene works. One might equally well argue that the pleasures of the flesh and salacious descriptions of the female body were just as much part of the cultural context that preceded the age of French Classicism. Foul language, scatological descriptions and scenes of joyous fornication abound everywhere in the literature of the time: from Rabelais to Sorel's *Francion*. They constitute an essential part of the literary production of the period. Even Malesherbes, often caricatured as as some sort of mournful regent in the succession of great authors, is no exception to the rule. Indeed, descriptions of sexual activity were the object of a healthy and well-established trade, becoming marginalized and ousted from the market-place only with the arrival of a new, more codified and elitist conception of art.[2] It is perhaps at that moment that a form of modern pornography was born, which became a private and clandestine purchase and required secrecy. As far as we can ascertain, there were little or no public displays of pornography tolerated between the years 1650 and 1750 – that is to say, for the duration of Louis XIV's reign, a period when the licentious and rather risqué tones of La Fontaine's *Contes* were barely tolerated. As for the rest, it was limited largely to a cerebral, coded eroticism, whose presence can be detected in the famous scene of the ribboned cane from *La Princesse de Clèves*, or in the furtive and uneasy clamminess of the seraglio scenes in *Bajazet*.

And yet, behind that discreet and distancing curtain, pornographic literature as a specific and hidden form of writing, with its own rules and generic conventions to set it apart, was in the process of being born. Some of its classics date from that period: *Vénus dans le cloître ou La Religieuse en chemise* appeared in 1672, *Le Rut ou Pudeur éteinte* by Pierre Corneille de Blessebois in 1676, and the anonymous *L'Ecole des filles ou La Philosophie des dames* in 1655,[3] the last undoubtedly the first libertine *Bildungsroman*. It would take too much space to go into the arguments in full here, but let us posit that it was under Classicism that erotic literature was invented, with its rules of production, its means of dissemination and the modes of consumption. From that point it no longer participated in the mainstream of writing, as it did in the time of Rabelais or the other men of the Renaissance or of the pre-classical period, where it rubbed shoulders with accepted forms of literary practice, in a rumbustuous and natural innocence, where the reading of such literature was a recognized and accepted fact of cultural life.

Not that the goal of this study is to reconstruct some sort of paradise lost where free speech and free love reigned, a paradise that the rise of the State in its modern sense would have destroyed for ever. If we take account of the presence of licentious and obscene elements in the more militant and outspoken works of the Enlightenment, then we would have to speak of an eclipse that was rather more temporary and less clearly defined than such a reconstruction might lead us to suppose. The sixteenth century also knew its moments of strict Church censorship. Neither the Reformation on the one hand nor the Counter-Reformation on the other did very much to encourage a discourse exalting the body and the pleasures of physical love. However, religious censure proved powerless to stem and control a tradition inherited from the Middle Ages and that also drew strength from a new naturalism. All the more so that medieval religion gave the body a space and a legitimacy which would be little by little denied to it.

An eclipse it was and a partial one without doubt, but one that was no less essential, for it was to create a genre and give a particular cultural status to obscene literature. Nothing could ever be the same again after it was thus driven underground. However much the philosophical teachings of the eighteenth century may have tolerated eroticism, it nonetheless continued to be the object of prohibition in society at large as well as in the civil courts. We thereby settled into a separation created by Classicism: between obscene literature, on the one hand, with its own distinct mode of operation and dynamics, so closely related to and yet so different from the literary evolution of recognized genres, and, on the other, a tolerance, which varied in degree over time, for the licentious and the allusive in general literary practice, where nonetheless obscenity and literature could never be reconciled as a result of the slow accretions of a pornographic tradition and censorship. The eclipse of Classicism lead to an evolution from a real and possible cohabitation to a radicalism that divided literature from pornography and made very few allowances in either direction.

This does not mean that pornographic literature was radically divorced from the more generalized forms of literary practice, or that no one ever thought to claim certain pornographic texts for the canons of literature to be judged by aesthetic rather than moral or judicial criteria. It is quite evident that the obscene and the salacious – to take two terms that would allow us to separate literature that is quite specifically pornographic from that which simply shows some obscene or, to a lesser degree, licentious, elements in an otherwise recognized literary genre, and whose end-result is not simply pornographic – imply two different modes of reading. On the one hand we have a literature of transgression, linked to a demand that is among other things extra-cultural in origin, in a relation to the text that entails complete and total alienation from the rest of society, and on the other a reading founded on cultural complicity, on shifts and subtle plays between the licit, the recognized and that which is forbidden and yet tolerated.

TRADE AND POLICING

It would be wrong to argue that the eighteenth century was a Golden Age of erotic literature.[4] At first sight, the approach is more quantitative than qualitative. All the facts seem to fit: the catalogue *L'Enfer de la Bibliothèque nationale*, the list of those held in the Bastille by *lettre de cachet*, calls to order issued by both civil and religious authorities – everything points to the scale on which erotic literature was produced and circulated.[5] We will limit ourselves to a few cases, and attempt to assemble a body of working assumptions in an area where nothing is ever clearly and explicitly stated. Indeed, it would be very difficult to measure the production of books that escaped censorship and which were circulated quietly and discreetly, to the point that they escaped either detection or control.

First of all there were the tutelary authorities. Throughout the eighteenth century measures were taken in order to strengthen or adapt the control that the chief of police and the director of the book trade exercised over the presses, the book shops and the hawkers.[6] These were targeted largely at Jansenist publications, which seem to have been a thorn in the side of the establishment for a long time.[7] Numerous decrees were promulgated by the Council (1701, 1706, 1716, 1731, 1732, 1744, etc.), and declarations were made in 1707 and 1717, all intended to strengthen the arsenal of repressive measures available to the authorities. Much revolved around the bull *Constitutio Unigenitus*, by which Clement XI condemned the 101 propositions suspected of being Jansenist drawn from the *Réflexions morales*, and thus reflects conflicts between the Catholic Church and the Jansenists on the one hand and between the papal and civil authorities on the other. Nothing seemed to put an end to it: Jansenism remained a perceived threat until quite late in the century, and registers of *lettres de cachet* in the Bastille show that printers and hawkers were still being arrested on charges of Jansenism long after 1750. These charges were much more common than those relating to the printing and dissemination of works thought to be offensive to accepted standards, or which were likely to 'disturb minds and threaten peace and order'.

From the middle of the century, more exactly dating from a decree of 1744, very few new measures were put in place to modify the rules governing the book trade. Not that the legal dead wood was entirely cleared away, but rather things became more a matter of habit and accommodation. As Malesherbes himself noted, the authorities began to turn a blind eye to fraudulent practices, seemingly resigned to not being able to control the circulation of seditious writings as strictly as they would like. Parlements grew weary, and smugglers enjoyed considerable success in crossing the frontiers undetected and in penetrating the

ports and the toll-houses. Everything seemed to be open to nego-
tiation: the choice of the censor, tacit permission for want of
actual authorization and the granting of a *privilège*, and even
complicity between the authorities and philosophical movements
as in the case of the *Encyclopédie*, saved by Malesherbes himself
after Damiens' attempt on the life of Louis XV, along with a
certain awareness that the meticulous enforcement of censorship
ran counter to the interests of the corporation of booksellers and
printers and thus against the economic interests of the realm.
As Diderot stresses in his *Mémoire sur la liberté de presse*, any
measure taken against the free circulation of books favours the
interests of foreign presses who print and distribute what France
bans.[8] It does not appear that the erotic literature benefited from
this relative permissiveness from the book trade. If anything,
the contrary seems to have been the case. Since they could not
pursue those books that dealt with radical philosophical issues or
contained anti-religious material, it appears that the powers that
be turned their attentions to lascivious works, by a rather pre-
dictable mechanism of transfer and compensation. Malesherbes'
position is exemplary from this point of view: tolerant of frivolous satirical works and yet strict on obscenity. This was part of
official policy without any doubt whatsoever, to which a variety
of declarations bear eloquent testimony, such as that of 10 May
1728: 'Experience has shown that, in spite of the vigilance and
care of the magistrates, a number of printers have gone as far
as to print, without *privilège* or permission, books that might
corrupt the morals of our subjects or to spread maxims that are
equally contrary to public order and religion.'[9] The inspectors
whose task it was to keep a watch over the 125 hawkers and the
40 bill-stickers in Paris also managed to keep an eye on cranks
and the authors of obscene publications. The records kept by
inspector d'Hémery attest to this very well indeed.[10] They therefore
attempted to arrest Chevrier not for his *Testament politique du
Maréchal de Belle-Isle*, but rather for two smaller works: *Le
Colporteur* and *La Vie du Père Norbert*. Only his death in 1762
put an end to their attempts to extradite him from Holland.
Fougeret de Montbron was not so lucky: found guilty of being

the author of *Margot la ravaudeuse* (1750), he was arrested on the request of the French ambassador in Amsterdam and transferred to the Bastille. His attacks on Voltaire and the anglomania of the philosophers did not protect him from the secular authorities. Despite also the relative leniency that they showed in other cases, the state did not hesitate to imprison hawkers caught in possession of engravings or obscene literature. In the case of reoffenders, the sentences could be as high as five years in the galleys. The same penalties applied to printers, as can be seen from the declaration of 10 May 1728.[11]

Concern to combat obscenity was what was demanded of the censors, who were asked to be attentive to the demands of decency in their reading of manuscripts. However, it is another question as to whether we can believe that the books offended the judgement of the censors themselves. In 1768 the attorney general, Joly de Fleury, recalled this in defining those matters 'in which one must be protected from authors'.[12] Thus, throughout the century, the powers that be did not cease to worry about the works that were being published either abroad or in Avignon, concerning which a memo from the directorate of the book trade noted, 'One might well be surprised that one would dare to print such infamy [*Le Portier des Chartreux* and *Thérèse philosophe*] under an ecclesiastical government and the eyes of the Inquisition itself. However, one would be less surprised to find that under this government, which is so despotic towards the people, the nobility is quite free and quite despotic in its turn, and that the highest nobles in Avignon allow the very printers responsible for such things to set up the presses in their own houses, and that there they do whatever they wish without fear of the Inquisition or the government.'[13] Powerless to act in Avignon, the book trade pursued those books that were introduced into France through the fair at Beaucaire. In 1766 d'Hémery seized 400 volumes contrary to religion or morality out of a total of 1,200 contained in packages belonging to five booksellers from Avignon. In France itself, a special watch was kept on Rouen, where a number of printers specializing in underground literature, whether pornographic or anti-religious, operated. They added works of their own to those imported from Holland or Neufchâtel. Thanks to the work of Robert Darnton, we know of the important role played by the Société Typographique de Neufchâtel in the diffusion of all sorts of forbidden literature, whether anti-religious or obscene.[14] The orders of the booksellers, which had a brisk turnover, and the letters of those who corresponded with the society prove the scale of the trade in erotic books and the success that it enjoyed in sales to the general public. It has been noted that there was more of a public for erotic literature than for works of philosophy. Buyers came from all levels of society: magistrates, junior officers in the guard (who seemed to prefer *Les Putains errantes* and *L'Ecole des filles*, if the archives are to be believed), and also nobles such as monsieur Dufort, the Master of Ceremonies, and M. de Fleury, son of the very attorney general who took such an interest in the censoring of evil works – all of whom, as we can tell, were happy to pay the market price for *La Science publique des filles du monde*.[15]

In *Le Tableau de Paris*, Louis-Sébastien Mercier has detailed the success that obscene publications and engravings enjoyed.[16] Nowhere was spared. They were sold on thoroughfares and places where prostitutes plied their trade, such as the Palais Royal, the entry to the Tuileries, the Opéra, and even more outrageously in the courtyard of the Hôtel de Soubise, and in the most popular and fashionable of cafés. One of the main places in which these forbidden books were sold was Versailles: not only in the town, which had several private booksellers, but also in the château itself and in the park. An inspection carried out in 1749 revealed that there were erotic books everywhere, from the apartments of the highest nobility to the little room of a preacher's servant.[17] On 14 March 1749 Lacasse Jean, a kitchen boy at the royal court, was taken to the Bastille on the authority of a *lettre de cachet* for having 'placed in the royal chapel at Versailles a complete edition of *Le Portier des Chartreux*'. He remained in the fortress until 1 October 1750. On 17 May it was the turn of Marcel de Gamaches, a master binder (released on 9 July), for having placed another copy of *Le Portier des Chartreux* in the château of Versailles.[18]

The sellers of such forbidden books followed the court on its way when it went to Compiègne. They set up their stalls at the annual fair in the park at Saint-Cloud, or found a place at the entry to the basilica at Saint-Denis, which as a religious foundation was exempt from the interference of the inspectors sent out by the directorate general of the book trade. The provinces did not escape from this illicit but fruitful trade either. There was many a bookshop at La Rochelle or Langres that would sell works of piety at the same time as the classics of erotic literature.[19] The hawkers here, like those in Paris, were bold and active, seeking out their customers in their homes, taking orders and sending for the rarest and most obscure works from Switzerland or Holland. Certain bookshops-cum-printers in the provinces, such as Besongne, Pierre and Robert Machual at Rouen, Renault at Lyons, Michelin at Provins and Hovius in Saint-Malo, were among the main ones to supply Paris with forbidden works.

The examination of the *lettres de cachet* at Paris, according to the list established by F. Funck Brentano at the beginning of the century, allows us to assess the growth in the trade of erotic books from another perspective. There are very few letters against people convicted of pornography sanctioned by *lettre de cachet*. Indeed, there are few instances of arrests for the crime of pornography, as far as we can tell from the records, between 1715 and 1731. In 1716 there was the apprehension of de Canelle (or Du Canel) under a charge of 'painting indecent figures on snuffboxes'. Then in 1718 there was the case of Jean Malassis, a bookseller and printer, imprisoned for selling prohibited books, which took the form of political tracts such as *La Polysynodie* or *Les Remontrances du Parlement de Paris faites au Roy en 1718*, erotic texts such as *L'Ecole des filles*, or hybrids of the two such as *Les Amours de Louis le Grand et de Mademoiselle du Trou*. In 1721 Jean Hubert, a painter, was arrested 'for having drawn plates that were contrary to religion, the State and public morals'. The crime of pornography, taking into account the limits on the use of *lettres de cachet* as evidence, was still relatively rare. And yet arrests for crimes linked to the book trade were numerous, although these were mostly for Jansenist propaganda: two in 1716, four in 1718, six in 1720, ten in 1721.

This growth in the number of arrests on such charges continued to such a point that all the offences relating to book-selling in the years 1726 to 1729 were connected with Jansenist propaganda. In 1729 the *Nouvelles ecclésiastiques* were creating a storm and large numbers of printers and hawkers were arrested, both professionals and political activists. From 1729 onwards we find that mixture that seems so odd in this day and age of the erotic and the philosophical, or of erotica and lampoons supporting those appealing against *Constitutio Unigenitus*. It seems that the fact that a book is banned is more of an issue for both readers and publishers, and that considerations of subject matter are secondary. Thus on 27 July 1729, Martin Baudrier, known as Deschaises, was arrested near Rouen by officials of the ministry of agriculture leading a horse loaded with banned literature. They were 'works contrary to religion and morality'. Baudrier was later sentenced, on 30 March the following year, to the iron collar and three years of imprisonment. On 16 November 1729 it was the turn of Jeanne Journal, who was held until 5 January 1730 for the distribution of 'Jansenist publications and of publications against the State and morality'. In 1730 there were nine arrests for offences related to book-selling, all connected with charges of Jansenism.

If charges relating to Jansenist propaganda were attested in large numbers between 1733 and 1760, when the last of the convulsionaries were being arrested, there was nonetheless a significant minority of arrests on charges relating to obscene publications: those hawking Jansenist literature, such as Dumény or Chartier (also known as 'the abbot'), and all those who engraved both 'Jansenist and obscene etchings', such as Nicolas Godochesnne, a young churchman, or Benoît Thévenard and his brother Antoine (also known as 'the dwarf'), a printer of line engravings arrested on 25 September and released on 6 June 1733, or Jean Diacre, 'a painter of miniatures', or last of all Henry Claude Maucourt, master sculptor, held from 29 September to 22 May 1733. The rhythm was then established and the years rolled on with a mixture of arrests for Jansenism and for obscenity, with a steady, but very clear rise in the number of secret printing works (the cases of the rue Saint-Séverin and the rue Meslay in 1736, the rue des Rats and the rue des Amandiers in 1737, and the rue de Lourcine in 1738); in these cases it is not entirely clear what sort of merchandise they were producing. From 1740 onwards the situation becomes clearer: we learn that the secret printing shop near the Arsenal was printing both obscene and Jansenist material: pages from both the *Nouvelles ecclésiastiques* and *Frétillon*. Along with the journeyman printers and the hawkers was also arrested a certain Jérôme Le Couteux, 'author of rather free works and of lampoons'. There is a clear mixing of genres and no potential source of profit is left untapped. In December 1740 there were a large number of arrests of printers of pornographic literature. On 17th, the hawker Auchereau was apprehended, to be transferred to Bicêtre on 7 January 1741, for 'the sale of obscene works, among them *Dom B . . ., portier des Chartreux*'. The same day was arrested Denis, a printer, who, in a secret printing shop, was printing 'copies of *L'Almanach de Priape* and other works contrary to morality'. On 19th, it was the turn of Pierre-Charles Canot, who was arrested and transferred to Bicêtre for having 'engraved plates from the *Almanach de Priape*'. In 1741, out of 40 *lettres de cachet* relating to crimes concerning book-selling, 22 were for the sale of pornography. The great scandal of the year was *L'Art de foutre*, attributed to Baculard d'Arnaud, who was arrested on 17 February and taken to Saint-Lazare on 14 March. The printer, Sulpice de Gamaches, was arrested on 29 January, along with the hawkers Laurent-Charles Guillaume and Jean Louis Tinel, who had been selling for him, and Joseph-Marie Anne d'Urey d'Harnancourt de Morsan, who had financed the operation (arrested on 23 February). These arrests clearly broke up a complex network. The authorities, put on the alert by the upsurge in the number of obscene publications, become more vigilant. On 28 February they arrest Blangy, a tapestry maker, who was taken to Bicêtre on 17 May 'for having engraved plates for *Dom Bougre*'; and Philippe Lefebvre, who was charged with having commissioned the plates, was arrested on the 28th. Those engaged in its diffusion as well as the hawkers were targeted. Blaud was arrested on 3 March, Marie Ollier on the 10th, and abbot Charles de Noury, the sacristan of the third order of Cluny, was detained on 14 April for selling. Louis Brullot was arrested on the 20th of the same month 'for having sold, despite a promise to desist from doing so, printed works, among which was *Dom Bougre*'.

Repressive measures having perhaps borne some fruit, there were no cases of pornography in 1743–4: a watch was kept on Jansenists and the distributors of political lampoons. In 1746 the pursuit of licentious works was on again. The binder Le Tellier was arrested on 10 July for having sold *Dom Bougre, Les Anecdotes de la chasse*, and was caught in possession of *nouvelles à la main, Les Trois voluptés, La Verité des miracles de Saint Pâris*, La Fontaine's *Les Contes*, and more. We know that in 1749 there were numerous searches carried out in Paris and even in Versailles.

It would be nice to be able to follow through year by year the various cases involving licentious works, and to be able to detect a continual growth, some sign of the proliferation of erotic and obscene literature, and the proof of its success. This project would be impossible for several reasons, however. First of all, obscene publications were not a separate category as far as those who were responsible for the regulation of the book trade were concerned: the notion of banned books applies to political satires, erotic literature and philosophical works. The tendency to confuse the defence of public order and the profit that they brought in was something of which not only the readers but also the printers, the hawkers and even the authorities were guilty. Only a publication such as *Le Canevas de Paris, ou Mémoires pour servir à l'histoire de l'hôtel du Roule*, in 1750, which led to the arrest of those suspected of being the authors – Barthélémy, François and Joseph Moufle d'Angerville, as well as Rochon de Chabannes (taken to the Bastille on 29 August) – or the careful search for copies of *Thérèse philosophe* from 1748 onwards, the year of its publication by Argens, received some sort of serious attention from the directorate of the book trade.[20]

We should also note that certain cases in particular (Damiens' assassination attempt, the expulsion of the Jesuits and the le Collier affair, for example) mobilized the inspectors, a tendency that became more and more apparent after 1757. In 1757 there were seventeen *lettres de cachet* relating to Damiens and his suspected accomplices, some cases of Jansenists that were thought to be involved in the affair, but, for the most part, the arrest of those responsible for defamatory satires, remarks against the person of the king and the diffusion of banned books which, for this period, consisted mainly of philosophical or anti-religious works. There was one sole case of offence against public morals that did not involve printed matter. On 10 April 1759 Pierre Michel Hérissant, a lawyer, was arrested and accused of being a *convulsionnaire*. Oddly, the charge specified that 'Hérissant was the creator of the sect, and responsible for enrolments. In their meetings, the brothers and sisters went naked. He was also the author of the "caisse des p . . .", an account created by the fees required from each of the new members and which paid for the prostitutes who were to provide pleasure for the brethren.' The use of the term *convulsionnaire*, to judge from this list of M. Hérissant's, activities, seems rather out of place. There was a similar refocusing of the activity of the inspectors during the expulsion of the Jesuits, where there were a number of arrests of people found distributing 'pamphlets favourable to the Jesuits'. In 1764 there were about 20 or so *lettres de cachet* relating to these sorts of offences alone.

The third factor that would make it impossible to carry out a survey of legal action against licentious writings was the increasingly prominent role played by pornography in political lampoonery. The turning-point seemed to come around 1765 with the arrest of Louis, Auguste and François Dieudé from Saint Lazare, for having made 'foul utterances against the king', a crime that earned them exile to Brittany. Under this heading of 'propos abominables', 'mauvais propos', which became more and more common, is probably hidden a language that is both pornographic and scatological in nature, and which is targeted at the person of the king, his policies and his mistresses, and which fed the *nouvelles à la main* – by which we should understand the sort of handwritten news-sheets, filled with unfounded rumours and the most injurious political denunciations. These circulated on an irregular basis in the streets of Paris, and there was no end to the arrests of those found distributing or writing them. In 1769 Jeanne-Jacqueline Pin (known as Dupin) from Laye was taken to the Bastille 'for having fabricated letters and stories where the name of Madame Adélaïde was compromised'. In 1770 Lamy and Kauffman were arrested for having circulated *nouvelles à la main*. In 1771 the records of Parlement business show clearly the fusion of scabrous and political material that was becoming typical: on 2 March Pierre-Athanase-Nicholas Pépin de Grouhette was arrested for 'licentious works advocating the disbanding of the Parlement'; he was freed on 3 December. With the start of the reign of Louis XVI, the production of these sorts of licentious satires continued unabated. In 1776 the majority of crimes relating to the book trade involved *nouvelles à la main*, whose style should be now be entirely familiar. In 1777 Jean-Baptiste-Jacques Lefebvre, a bookseller selling on the main staircase in the château of Versailles, was arrested on 19 September for having sold 'satires which contained insults and calumnies against the queen'. He was condemned to an exile of 30 leagues from the court on 17 April 1778. In the 1780s a new reason for imprisonment appeared: defamation, by which we should understand the writing and circulation of foul-mouthed and pornographic satires against the queen and ministers (*Les Amours du Vizir Vergennes; Les Petits soupers de l'hôtel de Bouillon*, among others). This was the charge laid against Mme La Touche de Gotteville, arrested on 24 May, and then again against Pascal Boyer, editor at the *Mercure de France*, who was at first suspected and then cleared of having been the author of defamatory satires against various prominent persons which had been published abroad. The le Collier affair encouraged the growth of the genre. In 1786 arrests became more and more frequent, both of hawkers and printers working underground, and against those booksellers distributing pamphlets attacking the honour of the queen and the virility of the king. If erotic works continued to be written, disseminated and read (on

30 June 1783 François Mallet, a bookseller from Neufchâtel, was arrested, of whom it is known 'that he paid M. the count of Mirabeau the sum of 100 Louis for the manuscript of his *Erotika Biblion*'), then it was no longer the main target of the censors, either. Political satires, whether compounded by pornographic material or not, were of more immediate concerns to the powers that be. In these troubled times there were far more urgent matters requiring attention than the defence of standards of decency.

In the meanwhile, it was true that pornography, and especially the erotic pamphlets devoted to the queen (such as the well-known *Les Amours de Charlot et de Toinette*, 1779), were a part of the general movement towards the desacralization of the monarchy. The queen was soiled, if only in the imagination of her subjects, mixed in with the most sordid foursomes, and offered up to the desires of those who read such satires. This if anything was a sign of the crisis facing the Ancien Régime. After the storm broke the freedom of the press was rapidly established. On 4 August 1789 the Constituant Assembly decided to abolish the system of *privilèges*, and thus the requirement for authorization of both authors and presses disappeared. On the 24th of the same month freedom of expression and thought were sanctioned by decree. There followed an explosion of pornographic and filthy pamphlets,[21] both revolutionary and counter-revolutionary. On the one hand there were works such as *L'Autrichienne en goguette ou l'Orgie royale; Le Godemiché royal, Les Soirées amoureuses du Général Mottier et de la belle Antoinette* and *Les Fureurs utérines de Marie-Antoinette, femme de Louis XVI*, while the counter-revolutionaries produced texts such as *Les Enfants de Sodome à l'Assemblée nationale, Vie privée et publique du ci-derrière marquis de Villette, citoyen rétroactif* (1790) and *La Requête et décret en faveur des putains, des maquerelles et des branleurs*. The list for the revolutionary period is long indeed. All parties were tarred with the same brush, and depicted in works that were either filthy or pornographic, everyone from the aristocracy to the Jacobins, from the émigrés to the Feuillants, from juring priests to Girondins, from the heroes of the Revolution to the actors in those theatres that sprang up with the end of the theatrical monopoly that had existed under the Ancien Régime, from the prostitutes in the Palais-Royal to members of Parlement of all persuasions. The massacre, the erotic show, the heavy-handed denunciations, couched in the crudest terms imaginable, knew no bounds. The fashion lasted until the days of the Consulate, culminating in the publication of the infamous pamphlet *La France foutue.*

The entry of the erotic into the political arena, and the easily measurable growth of pornography, are without doubt a product of those uncertain and troubled times, where there was a perceptible blurring and erosion of values. It can also be linked to changes in the literary world. From 1760 onwards, we know that there were a whole range of callings and people making their living in the world of letters. As Robert Darnton has shown, there then formed a sort of marginalized literary Bohemia, seeking work that was in harmony with its aspirations and its education. People from all orders took up the pen: freelance journalists, pamphleteers seeking protectors and causes to serve, courtiers working in the book trade, touts working for the Société Typographique de Neufchâtel, middlemen running between the booksellers in France and in Holland, England or Switzerland. There was a great temptation for anyone who could write to put together some erotico-political pamphlet to some foreign publisher or even to offer them directly to the political authorities, in a form of extortion. We know therefore that Théveneau de Morande, who published the journal *Le Gazetier cuirassé*, edited the pamphlet *Les Mémoires secrets d'une femme publique* against Madame du Barry, in four volumes, illustrated with engravings, and then sent a few of the more choice pages to the chancellor Maupéou, declaring that he would publish the pamphlet if a high price was not paid for his silence. Beaumarchais was sent to London in March 1774 to negotiate to buy back his manuscript from the pamphleteer, who was threatening to print and distribute a run of several thousand copies. Beaumarchais, acting in the name of the minister, had to pay for the destruction of the work, the price coming to 32,000 livres, and a pension of 4,000 for Théveneau, half of which would be revertible to his wife. *Les*

Mémoires secrets d'une femme publique were burned, it is claimed, in a brick oven.

The young writers belonging to this literary Bohemia were fascinated by the idea of a literary career, and often had no other recourse than to submit some sort of pornographic manuscript, which would sell well and which could reach a wide audience. Such was the case for Mirabeau, who was interned in the Bastille, and who, for want of money and something to occupy himself, gave to a Swiss editor the *Erotika Biblion* and *Ma conversion ou Le Libertin de qualité*. But there were others such as the Chevalier de la Morlière, who in 1748 published *Les Lauriers ecclésiastiques ou Les Campagnes de l'abbé de T.*, or Meusnier de Querlon, author of *Sainte Nitouche ou Histoire galante de la tourière des Carmélites* (1770), which was an attempt to produce a female rival to Le *Portier des Chartreux*, or yet again Pierre-François Tissot, who was sent to the Bastille for his *Capucinière ou Le Bijou enlevé à la course* in 1780. Last but not least we could cite the cases of Mercier de Compiègne and of Nougaret.[22]

What is rather more interesting than the case of these bohemians forced by poverty into writing pornography, and whose choice merely proves the success that obscene literature enjoyed at the period, is the case of those authors who were more or less well known and who eventually gave in to the temptation to produce erotic literature. Such was the case of Sénac de Meilhan, an administrator at Aunis, who hoped to rise as high as the rank of minister, and who, in parallel with his work as a philosopher, economist and novelist, published in 1775 a poem in six cantos entitled *La Foutromanie*. One might also cite the case of Alexis Piron, a lawyer who began his career at the bar in Dijon, and who wrote his *Ode à Priape* in 1710, gave up the law for the career as a man of letters; alongside his successful *Le Métromane*, he also produced other obscene works such as *L'Etymologie de l'Aze-te-foute*, *Le Désagrément de la jouissance*, *Leçon à ma femme* and so on, which all formed part of his collection, the *Oeuvres badines*.

Suffice it to say that the quantity of erotic works published shows that the genre had achieved a success and a notoriety that it had never enjoyed before. In conclusion, we might give two additional proofs. First of all, there is the recognition of the existence of such a kind of writing, both within its own world and outside. Just as any utopia implicitly or explicitly refers to More, to Campanella and to Plato, so erotic literature refers back to its classics also: the works of 'L'Arétin' (Pietro Aretino), *Dom Bougre* or *Thérèse philosophe*. These appear either in the preface or thereafter as a source, as the point of origin for a literary line, as the archetype for a genre – or it may be that reading them constitutes a decisive moment in the education of the hero. This presence, either at a narrative or a referential level, is the proof of a certain cultural status, of a certain historicity, and indeed of a hierarchy in the canon of erotic works. Chevrier's *Le Colporteur* conveniently evokes the assortment of rather questionable literature that the salesmen of this most sought-after commodity carried with them. There is virtually no erotic novel that does not refer back to other works in the genre: from *L'Education de Laure* to *La Vie de Monsieur Nicolas*. When Rameau's nephew attacks false and hypocritical shows of virtue by evoking the unspoken desires of an apparently prudish woman, it is the pornographic novel that provides him with his language, convinced that a reference whose source will be immediately recognizable is worth more than a long explanation.

> And what of that woman who mortifies her flesh, who visits prisons, who attends all meetings organized for charity, who walks with downcast eyes, and would not dare look a man in the eye, ever on guard against the temptations of the senses. Does any of this keep her heart from burning or stop her sighs, or her flaming obsessing her? Her imagination at night rehearses the scenes of the *Portier des Chartrains* and the postures of Aretino.[23]

There would not be one contemporary reader of this text who would not have understood the allusion.

Many more such examples could be enumerated, and the various proofs, either referential or narrative, could easily be heaped up. Let us recall two important facts. We know from *Les*

Confessions that a woman named 'La Tribu' lent erotic books in that most prudish of cities, Geneva.

> However, if my good taste did not keep me from silly and insipid books my good fortune preserved me from such as were filthy and licentious: not that La Tribu, a woman in all respects most accommodating, would have made any scruple about lending them to me; but in order to increase their importance, she always mentioned them to me with an air of mystery that had just the effect of making me refuse them, as much from disgust as from shame.[24]

Let us last of all quote Diderot as a witness to public taste for erotic literature, and who, just like the Master in *Jacques le Fataliste*, does not cease to torment his valet in order to know every small detail of his past loves:

> MASTER: If Jacques wanted to give me very great pleasure . . .
> JACQUES: How might he go about that?
> MASTER: He would begin with the loss of his virginity.
> JACQUES: And why is that, if you please?
> MASTER: That is because, out of all the stories of the same type, it is the only interesting one. All the other times are nothing more than insipid banal repetition. Out of all the transgressions of a pretty woman, I am sure her father confessor is only interested in the first time.[25]

For the reader of *Jacques le Fataliste* and for the reader of the eighteenth-century novel, the Master is your brother! You cannot but recognize yourself in him, and indeed the author invites you to do so:

> And what is this, reader? One love story after another! That makes one, two, three or four tales I've told you, and three or four more still to come. That is a lot of love stories. It is also a fact that, since I am writing for you, I must either go without your applause or follow your tastes, and you have shown a decided taste for love stories. All of your works, whether in verse or prose, deal with love; nearly all your poems, elegies, eclogues, idylls, songs, epistles,

comedies, tragedies, operas are love stories. Nearly all your painting and statues are love stories. Love stories have been your only food ever since you existed, and you show no sign of growing tired of them.[26]

Replace 'love' with a slightly stronger or more precise term, and we would have a fairly accurate summary of eighteenth-century taste for erotic literature, and a further proof, if any were needed, of the success of the genre.

The list of titles can be found in the appendix. Because of their sheer number, and because of their referential value and the literary talents of their authors, we can perhaps begin to form a judgement of the scale of the trade in erotic fiction as well as of the importance of the genre, a genre that was doubtless very important in setting the tone for the period.

The Effects of Reading Erotic Literature

PICTORIAL REPRESENTATION: GHENDT'S *LE MIDI*

We will begin here with an analysis of a print by Emmanuel de Ghendt based on a gouache by P. A. Baudouin, entitled *Le Midi* (see figure 2.1). A young woman is stretched out on the mossy bank, her open parasol cast aside to her left. Behind her is a statue, a young man on a pedestal carved with cupids, with leaves climbing the sides of the trellises set around a circular clearing, rather reminiscent of the bull's eye of a target. We can tell it is noon, the time of siesta or midday nap, and though we might forget the young lady's expensive clothing (wig, corset, lace, skirt of watered silk, bracelets and ribbons), one might nonetheless be put in mind of Jean-François Millet's working sketches and paintings – *Bergère dormant à l'ombre d'un buisson de chênes* (pastel, Musée de Saint-Denis, Reims, dated to between 1872 and 1874) or *La Méridienne* (in the Museum of Fine Arts in Boston, 1866). We might therefore construct a series based on scenes of pastoral relaxation, going from the rather spicy drawings of the eighteenth century to the rustic naturalism of the nineteenth, without forgetting the series of erotic variations by Courbet (*Le Sommeil*, Musée du Petit-Palais, Paris), or the motif of the figure at rest used so often by Pablo Picasso. On closer inspection, it would be rather dangerous, even a complete falsification, to draw too many links between *Le Midi* and the pastoral tradition to which it seems to refer. There is nothing in Ghendt's print that recalls the

Figure 2.1 Le Midi, *print by Emmanuel de Ghendt after a gouache by
P. A. Baudouin (reproduced by kind permission of the
Bibliothèque Nationale, Paris)*

countryside. The decor is that of a carefully designed garden or a folly. There is no opening out onto the surrounding landscape, no movement towards the countryside on the horizon; rather, everything tends to give the impression of a closed space. Of course there is no hint of a siesta either. The young lady avoids the shade and has stretched herself out in the sunlight: by means of a patch of brilliant white sunlight the engraver calls our attention to this body, lying there in wanton abandon. Between the dark foliage and this body bathed in brilliant light there is the same harsh discord as between the naked model and her male companions in Manet's *Le Déjeuner sur l'herbe*. Everything here seems to point to and to underline the fact that the title is nothing but a trap, or rather that *Le Midi* exists only to justify the lighting effect employed, and that the eye should be drawn directly to that figure sprawled in the sunlight, to the whiteness of both her face and her breasts, to the dress that clings to her body and to the right hand that points to an object that she has dropped in the ground at her side: an open book. The eye is also drawn to her right leg, which follows on from the line of the body, and the fact that her feet are well apart, her left shoe dangling from her foot.

The model's eyes are open: two black points in a face that appears white in the sunlight. The mouth is half open, in a sort of fervid fixedness. The more we look at this face, the more we divide up black and white as the print invites us to do; we note that her gaze looks elsewhere, and is not focused on anything in particular, not even at the critic who looks at the image. She stares at an absent reality that she is perhaps the only one to see. The body, her body, is both tensed from the pelvic region to the head, and yet offered to the reader from the waist down to her shoes. One hand, the left, is hidden in her skirts, and, from the folds of the dress highlighted by the sunlight, it is quite clear where it is reaching.

The content of the picture is not hard to understand. In the shelter of the foliage growing over the trellises, in the middle of this aristocratic garden, and with the sun at its midday heat, a young lady is masturbating. The distribution of light and shade is nothing to do with reality; rather, it invites the spectator to look at this body, and to look beyond the surface appearances.

Her right hand, with its index finger stretched out, points to an object lying on the ground. It has not been put there, it has fallen, as if it had suddenly slipped from the fingers of the young reader. Hence the position of the book, half open with the spine upwards, all of which indicates that it is not simply part of the decor but rather an object that is in use, and that the young lady has read it. The way in which it is lying indicates without doubt that she has stopped at a particular page that has caught her attention, to the point that the book falls open almost automatically at the page. Everything is said. The abandoned book was a point of departure for her daydreams, and it is not hard to guess the content of those dreams. The cupids who push and jostle around the base of the statue confirm the reading if there was any doubt, as does the ironic smile of the beautiful young man that crowns the pedestal.

But let us look a little more carefully at Ghendt's print. The beautiful young man, the demi-god on the pedestal, a slightly more mature version of the cupids around the base but who nonetheless still retains the round cheeks of his youth, deprived of the arms and hands that were so useful elsewhere, is here reduced to a gaze. Not that the statue's eyes are empty: he is looking at the young lady, and one might even think that the statue was looking rather surprised through the bull's eye behind it at this spectacle of this young lady who believes herself to be alone and cut off from the world. The construction implied and carefully underlined is undeniable: the book is read and the illusion is taken for reality to the point of driving the young woman to what Rousseau was to call 'that dangerous supplement'. However, the only eroticism that the picture offers is that of the body offered up in the moment of orgasm, and which is the object of such an avid and penetrating gaze, without that gaze being felt, identified or even noticed.

Let us sum up what Ghendt's print tells us, or tells the person who looks at it. To read is to belong to that moment that precedes and calls for the most intimate of caresses, as the positioning and the gaze of the bust indicate, to be a voyeur of an act that is in itself that of incompleteness, of a substitute. We could go even further with the commentary on the print that both opens itself up and comments on itself. Let us give the picture the title it deserves and which corresponds to its message: 'The Effects of Reading', or 'The Influence of Wicked Books'. Thus a young lady reads a pornographic novel on her own and finishes as the victim of the desire to which the book gives rise, and which forces her to masturbation. We see the book abandoned, and the moment of climax sweeping through the body like a wave, as is indicated by the unusual tenseness of her position, the stiffness of her limbs, a certain absence in her manner, even by the detail of the shoe that has pulled away from the curve of her foot. Everything speaks of the power of the book, which is here exalted and magnified. An insignificant object, almost entirely abandoned, but which confers meaning on each of the elements in the composition. As much as to say that literature is not just an empty game here. Anyone who gives themselves up to it will be burned by its flames, and will be forced to follow those words with the inevitable gesture.

By the composition of the print and by the position that it imposes on the person that looks at it, Ghendt's work offers us an insight into how this violent effect results from reading. Everything turns on the gaze. The eyes do not read: they look. What provides the reader with the necessary information is not any caption, which would be wrong, but rather a setting, a certain organization, a picture, a tableau, an interplay of gazes between the *putti* and the statue, all of which converge on a single point: this body taken in its moment of most intense pleasure, of *jouissance*. However, the moment of pleasure is not just a solitary one: the bull's eye evokes the hidden, indiscreet gaze, the statue comes to life to watch, and the very sunlight points to what there is to see. The print is therefore a setting, a picture with this body in its moment, of that tensed pelvis, of that hidden hand, but yet so very present, to the very point of giving life to this abandoned body. The young lady reader depicted in *Le Midi*, the reader of erotic works and the lover of prints – all voyeurs together. There is no sensation to be had but by the intermediary of that gaze which steals in secret from those bodies seized by desire. *Le Midi*, by its theme, by its setting and by the position of the gaze that it imposes on the lover (of prints) demonstrates this very well indeed.

NARRATIVE SETTINGS: TISSOT, BIENVILLE, RÉTIF DE LA BRETONNE AND DIDEROT

The print is not the only form to demonstrate the effects of reading pornographic literature by its own means (here, distribution of light and shade, fragmentation, composition and the play of gazes between one element and another). Medicine, and especially sexual pathology, which was born during the Enlightenment, insisted on the role of badly chosen reading matter in the birth of excessive sexual desires. The role of such literature is underlined in texts such as Tissot's *L'Onanisme, dissertation sur les maladies produites par la masturbation*, which appeared in 1760, or in *La Nymphomanie ou Traité de la fureur utérine* by Bienville, published in 1771.[1] Bad servants and wicked books offer sufficient explanation for bad habits, a fact of which both doctors and confessors were thoroughly convinced. Penitential and confessional manuals pay attention to the importance of reading, and the censure can only be understood in relation to the literature that was tacitly implied, and to its (negative) influence. Obscene literature is denounced from every point of view: religious, medical and social. It is pursued or forbidden, convinced that it exerts a dangerous influence and leads to destructive excess, to the breaking of laws and to the sins of the flesh, to a sullying of the self on both physical and moral levels. The world appears united in its condemnation of this literature, which is exactly the paradox of this period where we see the book triumphing over all. Philosophers denounce books by fanatics, the Church denounces the writings of the philosophers and licentious works, while the artists, jurists and doctors all denounce those works that would incite debauchery and moral corruption or place the individual in conflict with the law. At a general level, all sides took it upon themselves to defend or damn the book, implying at each turn that it exerted an influence, for good or ill according to the case one happened to be arguing at the time. As for erotic literature, there is scarcely any need to refer to the authorities, for there are enough attestations of people's opinions. In *Les Confessions*, Rousseau wittily evokes the effects created by the reading of such licentious works when he referred to 'those dangerous books that a fine lady finds inconvenient, because they can only be read with one hand'.[2]

Novels of the time offer ample testimony to the effects of erotic literature. To this end I would cite at length the following astonishing extract from Rétif de la Bretonne's *Monsieur Nicolas*:

I have said that I was faithful to Zéphire with her companions. That truth might lead you into error. I must tell all if I am not to deceive you. Here then is another of my turpitudes, all the more surprising that it took place in a period of virtue and that nothing seemed to foreshadow it. It was a frightening storm in the middle of a period of calm, a terrible dream in a peaceful night . . . I was true to my intended and abstaining from other women. I was living more virtuously than I ever had done and thought that I could even become accustomed to it. But what is going to show the danger of books such as *Le Portier des Chartreux*, *Thérèse philosophe*, *La Religieuse en chemise* and others is the terrible and sudden lust that they excited in me after long abstinence! A great libertine, that Molet whom I have already mentioned and who was a fellow-lodger at Bonne Sellier's, had come to see me one Sunday morning when I was still in bed and brought me the first of these books, which I had only glimpsed at La Massé's. Filled with a lively curiosity, I took it eagerly and started reading in bed. I forgot everything, even Zéphire. After a score of pages, I was on fire. Manon Lavergne, a relative of Bonne Sellier, came on behalf of my former landlady to bring me my linen and Loiseau's, which Bonne continued to wash for us. I knew what Manon's morals were like after my adventure with her at her mother's house (and here I would only refer the reader to *La Drame de la vie*), along with the brothers of her mother's pupils. I threw myself on her. The young lady did not put up very much resistance.

I resumed my reading again after she had gone. Half an hour later, there appeared Cécile Decoussy, my sister Margot's companion, who came to me on her behalf to ask why she no longer saw anything of me. Without any regard for this young blondes position (she was about to be married), nor for the atrocious way in which I was bringing shame on my sister in the person of her friend, I put such fury into my attack that, alarmed as much as surprised, she thought that I had gone mad. She gave way, after having begged me on her knees to let her go. I took up my baneful reading once again.

About three quarters of an hour later. Thérèse Courbisson arrived, laughing and bantering: 'Where is he, that lazy scamp? Still in bed!' And she came over to tickle me. I was waiting for her. I seized her almost in mid air, like a feather, and pulled her under me with only one hand. 'Oh! And after what you've just done to Manon? A fine man you are!' She was caught before she could finish, and since she was very partial to physical pleasures, she did nothing more but help me. At last she tore herself from my arms when she heard my landlord coming upstairs . . . She went out, leaving the door open. I finished my book.

The bed had heated me up again, and the three pleasures I had enjoyed were just a spur to my senses. The violence that I had done only added to my ardour. I got up with the intention of seeking out Zéphire, bringing her back to my room and abandoning myself to my erotic frenzy. At that moment, somebody scratched at the door, which I had only pushed to. I started, thinking that it might be Zéphire. 'Who is it?' I shouted, 'Come in.' 'Séraphine', said a voice which I thought I recognized. I trembled, thinking that it was Séraphine Destroches, who had come to scold me for my behaviour with her companion, Decoussy. 'Who is it?', I repeated. 'Séraphine Jolon.' The only person I knew by that name was the housekeeper of a painter who was our neighbour in the rue de Poulies, and to whom I had whispered sweet nothings once or twice. But then Largeville turned up and Jeanette Demailly, and I left. Reassured, I opened the door. It was her . . . 'I have come', said the pretty girl, 'on behalf of Mlle Fagard, now Mme Jolon, my sister-in-law, who begs you to introduce me and recommend me to Mlle Delaporte, who thinks very highly of you, and who leads me to understand that you might be of service to me!' 'Immediately', I said to her. 'Be seated, fair neighbour.' She was charming! As she turned round, she showed her perfect figure to advantage. I seized her and threw her down onto the bed. She tried to defend herself, which merely threw oil on the fire. I did not even take the time to shut the door. I finished, I began again . . . 'I . . . did . . . not . . . tell . . . you . . .', gasped Séraphine, 'that . . . my sister-in-law . . . Jolon . . . was waiting for me.' The very idea drove me to a third bout and I was like a madman when somebody pushed open the door . . . It was Agathe Fagard, and, oh, how beautiful she was. 'Help me . . . ! Help me . . . !' cried Séraphine, entirely spent . . . I left her uncovered, and I threw myself at Fagard, pushing the door to with my foot and forcing the provocative little brunette onto my bed, and, while she was more astonished than overwhelmed, I submitted her to a sixth triumph no less vigorous than the first, carried away as I was by the fire of my imagination, more potent than even you, the satyrs . . .

. . . Such is the effect of erotic literature. And yet I know of a book even more dangerous than the ones I have just named, and that is *Justine*, a work that drives men to cruelties. Danton used to read it for the excitement it offered.[3]

The role of fantasy and exaggeration cannot entirely erase the belief that underlies this astounding extract from *Monsieur Nicolas*: namely, that obscene literature forces the reader to take some sort of action. Nothing can slow or stop its effects, neither heart nor body, neither moral nor physiological considerations. Everything happens as if the simple act of reading would be enough to renew a sexual desire that the physical act ought to have satisfied. The book appears to be stronger than any resolution, so that neither a 'period of virtue' nor the will to abstain will suffice. Reading the book is described as 'a frightening storm in the middle of a period of calm, a terrible dream in a peaceful night'. Nothing can resist it: neither resolve nor a period of abstinence: 'I was living more virtuously than I ever had done and thought that I could even become accustomed to it.' Reading excites curiosity and latent desires: 'I took it eagerly and started reading in bed . . . After a score of pages, I was on fire.' We may also note that the erotic work does not belong to the cultural order but rather to that of desire: 'I took it eagerly.' Read with passion, the effects are immediate: 'After a score of pages, I was on fire.' As much as to say that the effect of reading does not operate on a moral or psychological level, but rather on that of the physical. The desire for physical release is quite real and possesses the reader to the point that he appears transformed, ready to do anything to satisfy his ends. The first woman he sees is the first victim: 'I threw myself on her.' But the satisfaction is only temporary: the power of the book goes beyond any normal state of arousal, and indeed reality seems powerless to satisfy the desire that is born in the imagination. 'I resumed my reading again.' A new reading and a new victim. The effect of the work is to turn him into a madman: 'I put such fury into my attack that, alarmed as much as surprised, she thought that I had gone mad'. The act of reading leads directly to the act of rape. There is no more gallantry, no attempt to seduce, but rather an immediate desire that cares little for the consent or otherwise of the partner, rather the desire for release is of a different order altogether and takes precedence over everything. 'She gave way, after having begged me on her knees to let her go.' However, the desire for the pleasure of reading is confused with the desire for physical pleasure and remains as unsatisfied as ever, as Rétif de la Bretonne notes: 'I took up my baneful reading once again.' And it is this reading that multiplies his sexual powers by ten and allows him to attain a level of sexual potency without parallel or precedent: 'Oh! And after what you've just done to Manon? A fine man you are!' Even after this, Monsieur Nicolas remains unsatisfied and carries on with his reading, recognizing that the three previous climaxes had only whetted his appetite. The terms used – 'violence', 'erotic frenzy' and 'ardour' – convey the radical transformation, the process of bestialization that, paradoxically, gives him almost superhuman powers. There will be a fifth, and even a sixth victim, with whom his pleasure will be as intense as the first. Everything is the fruit of the imagination, and were he to cease to read, his desire would die away as rapidly as it had been aroused, which leads us to the obvious conclusion that it is reading that fuels the entire process: 'Such is the effect of erotic literature.' The narrator's comment comes almost as a moral, underlining the lesson to be drawn from the tale. For, apart from the fact that there is explicit approval given in the text to the hero's extraordinary virility, to which Rétif is quite happy to lay claim and to market, the hero of the passage is nonetheless the book itself, which trans forms the history of the reader under its influence into a sort of epic.

The extract from *Monsieur Nicolas* forms a confession of that which everyone is supposed to know: that erotic literature has the power to incite people to action and even to the point of madness. It breaks down physiological constraints to the point that his sexual excess knows no limits, as well as social and moral constraints: nothing can prevent the character from satisfying his desire, neither friendship, innocence, the absence of his partner, nor even the fear of being caught in the act (as we might note from the ever-open door). The man under the spell of the erotic work knows neither remorse nor pity: he requires physical satisfaction. He is unfaithful, and throws himself without discrimination on any partner that might present themselves. The book transports him to a different reality whose sole law is the desire that he must satisfy. 'I forgot everything, even Zéphire.' Reading the erotic text destroys the rational order, and the universe overbalances into the realm of an all-devouring passion. There is no question of choice or of any regard for the wishes of the other. The only language is that of *jouissance*.

Rétif de la Bretonne offers ample witness to the power of desire, but, above all, the power of a reading that exercises such a grip that none can escape from it. The book imposes a certain style of behaviour and abolishes choice. It moreover abolishes the past, replacing it with a present where the future is reduced, by that same desire, to a mere sketch or outline. The erotic work thereby destroys the mechanism of reading, which is essentially one of choice and of play in the system, imposing a monolithic model of behaviour. Incapable of satisfying the desire it engenders, it forces the reader to leave the realm of the imagination and impose the law of the book on the real world. If the assaults follow on one after another, then we are to see in this a particular obsession of Rétif's, a way of thinking that functions around accumulation and hyperbole, an allegorical narrative of a desire that is never satisfied but always rises again from the ashes like the phoenix, an attestation of the specific nature of the imagination at work in the reading process, an imagination stronger than the reality to which it refers.

The depiction of the effect of reading erotic literature does not always have such novelistic verve or (whether Rétif intended there to be any or not) the same degree of humour. When doctor Tissot, author of *De l'onanisme*, describes those patients in the last stages of consumption resulting from masturbation, he does not neglect to underline the influence of books in the development of the illness, even though he does not give precise details. His sense of narrative construction is used to describe the various morbid states and symptoms. Everything results from writing. Tissot is not unaware of the role of erotic literature in the birth of vice, recognizing that one of the best ways to cure those given to masturbation is to forbid them to read, especially those works 'which might remind them of certain ideas or objects that it would be better they forgot.'[4] The emphasis on the logic of taboo that is such a feature of Tissot's account is a long way from the exaltation of Rétif's tale. The scientific tone he adopts is at a far pole from that of the novel. The cause is understood and the conclusion is constructed in the form of a diagnosis: 'All I can say is that idleness, inactivity, remaining too long in bed, a bed that is too soft, a diet composed of succulent, flavoured and spicy foods, too much wine, questionable friends, and licentious works are all causes likely to lead people to such excesses, and that these things cannot be avoided with too much care.'[5] There is little to distinguish between Tissot's work and Bienville's *De la nymphomanie*. In the most sober and learned tones he refers the reader to the case of Lucile, a young lady from Lyons, underlining the importance of the books that she was reading (and indeed the ones she refused to read), and their function as both cause and symptom. 'Pious works of instruction cause her "the vapours" [a form of nervous reaction], and she reads nothing other than *Le Paysan parvenu*, or other works of that sort, all of which nourish in her veins the poisons and sad fires that consume her and in her mind the dangerous and foolish hopes that obsess her.'[6] We should note that the language of the novelists often has much more to offer in the way of insight than the cold and sententious pronouncements of the men of science writing on the same subject.

We need have no fear of tiring the reader with the enumeration of these examples, but we know moreover from Rétif and from numerous other sources that erotic literature was commonly offered to clients in the houses of prostitution of the Ancien Régime (and no doubt after that period also). Monsieur Nicolas recounts that on a visit to La Massé, a prostitute living on the rue des Frêtes, he was offered erotic literature 'with illustrations for the reader's amusement' to while away the time. 'It was rather cold that evening and so I sat by the big fire, on a sort of sofa, and took up the illustrated work. It was *D. B.* (*Dom Bougre, portier des Chartreux*), which I knew only by name at that time. I read it quickly, and I had got as far as Saturnin and Suzette looking through a gap in the partition at what was happening in Toinette's bedroom, when the door opened.'[7] The same type of scene can be found in *Margot la ravaudeuse,* in *Thérèse philosophe* or in *Le Rideau levé ou L'Education de Laure.* The erotic work as incitement is part of the ceremony of the houses of prostitution, and forms a necessary step in initiation scenes. It is by means of such works that novices in the trade learn their ABC, that clients prepare themselves 'aux jouissances' – for the pleasures to come, and that young, innocent readers experience the headiness of their first ardour. The narrative recounted by the 'historiennes' in the *Cent-vingt journées de Sodome* is merely a variation on the pedagogical and excitatory use of erotic literature so much a topos of other works in the genre.

The Reader as Voyeur

I have demonstrated and underlined the perceived power of the erotic novel, and given some indication both of how it functions and of the conditions and constraints that it imposes on the reader by means of sexual desire. What I would like to do now is to discuss the *mise en scène* of the erotic novel by means of a few examples. This is a procedure that we have already seen at work in the visual arts, as, for example, in the case of Ghendt's print.

Everything turns on the gaze: the reader must be made to see, for the book can give rise to the desire for *jouissance*, for pleasure, only by describing those bodies offered up to stimulate desire or by depicting the gestures and postures of the moment of climax itself. Therein lies the origin of its own tension, its strange and undeniable power.

By way of introduction we will look at Marivaux's *Le Paysan parvenu*. The hero, Jacob, is a countryman who has come to the city. He is a solid and rather sly young man always ready to profit from the things and the people he finds along the way, quick to seize the moment by an offer of help, by replying to a smile, by rejoining in banter, by offering his muscular arm to a lady overcome while crossing the Pont-Neuf, or by putting his sword to help a man who was being attacked. It is the story of social promotion, where Jacob rises from domestic service to wealth through the love of women and the support of great men. For Jacob inspires tender feelings and very real desires in the women he meets. The freshness of his physique, his rustic ingenuousness, on which he plays a good deal, and his association with the countryside, all of which seem to promise a certain vigour in love that moral education and social niceties have eroded in other men, furthermore seduces and appeals to experienced and discerning women. Le *Paysan parvenu* is also the story of an initiation and apprenticeship in love. Jacob learns to love and to refine his tastes and desires, and the book presents a narrative of the feminine body as blazon. Jacob first of all discovers the beauty of a bosom (that of the financier's wife) seen through the scooping neckline of a low-cut dress, and then the beauty of a leg that shows its fine line under a skirt lifted slightly too far.

In its own way, *Jacques le Fataliste*, through the mouth of Jacques himself, shows that the exhibition of the body is the means to inspire desire, the setting of the scene for an embrace that is designed to be seen. I will cite the story of Jacques' involvement with Dame Suzon, surprised by the priest:

> JACQUES: I was in Suzon's barn alone with her.
> MASTER: And you hadn't gone in there for nothing.
> JACQUES: No. Then the priest arrived, lost his temper, started preaching and asked Suzon haughtily what she thought she was doing alone with one of the most debauched boys in the village in the most isolated part of the farm.
> MASTER: I can see that you had a reputation even then.
> JACQUES: And well earned at that. He was really rather angry and added a few even less flattering things to what he had said already. So then I got angry. From swapping insults it turned to blows. I grabbed a pitchfork and passed it between – one prong through here and the other here – and then threw him into the hayloft, not more or less but exactly as if he were a bale of hay.
> MASTER: And how high was this hayloft?
> JACQUES: Ten feet at least. And he couldn't get down without breaking his neck.
> MASTER: And after that . . . ?
> JACQUES: Next I undid Suzon's blouse, took her breasts, caressed them, she resisted a little. In the barn there was a pack saddle, whose other uses were well known to us. I pushed her onto it.
> MASTER: You pulled up her skirts?
> JACQUES: I pulled up her skirts.
> MASTER: And the priest could see all that?
> JACQUES: As I see you now.
> MASTER: And he shut up?
> JACQUES: Certainly not, if you please. Barely able to contain his anger, he started shouting: 'Mmm . . . mm . . . murder! Fff . . . ff . . . fire! Ttt . . . tt . . . thief!' and then the husband, whom we thought far away, ran in.[8]

Everything is in place. Especially the erotic tableau organized around the gestures of the couple, the gaze that sees them without being able to participate in their pleasure, except in his desire. That the spectator should be a priest in this case is of little importance. And is he as strict as his position might give us to understand? Diderot takes care to describe him 'shouting, swearing, foaming at the mouth, struggling with his head, his feet, his hands, with his whole body, and quite ready to throw himself from the top of the barn',[9] or again, 'He was a sort of dwarf, hunchbacked, gnarled, blind in one eye, with a stammer, jealous and lecherous, in love with and maybe even loved by Suzanne. He was the village priest.'[10] Everything is quite clear from here on in. Jacques sets in motion the narrative organization that will give rise to desire: exhibition and the gaze, here solicited rather than as an intrusion. All the important information has been conveyed. The language of *jouissance*, absent here, is rendered useless, and it is articulated in *Jacques le Fataliste* only by plays on words and other witticisms:

> I was beneath her, cutting on the slope. Suzanne bent her legs, drawing her heels up against her thighs. Since she had pulled her knees up, her skirts didn't come down very far. I was still cutting on the slope hardly looking where I was hitting and missing most of the time. At last, Suzanne spoke: 'Jacques, you will finish soon, won't you?'
>
> And I replied: 'Whenever you want, Madame Suzanne.'
>
> 'Can't you see that I want you to finish?' she said in a low voice. So I finished, got my breath back and finished again. And Suzanne . . .
>
> MASTER: Took away the virginity you never had?[11]

Many more examples of this type of rather witty writing where little is made explicit could be adduced. In the case of Justine: 'I don't know if I raped her, but I do know that I didn't do her any harm and she didn't do me any either.'[12] In the case of the master's encounter with Agatha: '. . . I let myself go, got into bed and was overwhelmed with caresses which I returned. There I was, the happiest man, and I still was when . . .'[13] All this is pretty poor stuff when compared with the depiction of those bodies offered or suggested to the gaze, with the setting of desire and expectation. There is not a reader who would forget the scene between Jacques and Denise. 'I took her by the arm and drew her closer to the edge of my bed. I took one of her feet and put it in the side of the bed, I raised her skirts up as far as her knee, where she held them down with both hands. I kissed her leg, and attached the garter which I had held on to, and hardly had I put it on when Jeanne, her mother, came in.'[14] Not to mention the evocation of that slow and sensual caress, apparently applied for medical purposes, that Denise, armed with a soft cloth, applied to Jacques' knee by way of physiotherapy:

> He still suffered from a terrible itching on his knee. Denise offered to comfort him and took a little piece of flannel. Jacques put his leg out of bed, and Denise started to rub below the wound with her flannel, first with one finger, then with two and then three, four and then with her whole hand. But it wasn't enough to have cured the itching under the knee and on the knee itself. It still needed to be cured above the knee as well, where he could feel it even more sharply. Denise put her flannel above his knee and started rubbing there quite firmly, first with one finger, then two, then three, then four, then her whole hand. Jacques had not stopped looking at her and his passion reached such a point that, no longer being able to resist any longer, he threw himself on Denise's hand . . . and then kissed her . . . hand.[15]

The final comment, full of innuendo, offered to the unsatisfied reader ('If you are not satisfied with what I have revealed to you of Jacques' loves, Reader, you may go away and do better – I consent to it')[16] prove that the main thing is not the possession, but rather that tension of desire.

It is this allusive quality that marks out *Jacques le Fataliste* as a work that demonstrates so well the workings of erotic literature, even if it does not enjoy the same reputation as something more typical of the genre, such as *Les Bijoux indiscrets*, whose standing as an erotic novel is much the superior of Diderot's works. The fiction behind *Les Bijoux* relies on a play on words that is allowed for by the use of erotic vocabulary, with the word jewels designating the sexual organs, as indeed can be the case in English. There is another jewel involved in the novel, this being Mangogul's ring, which has the effect of making the female genitalia of the women the hero encounters confess their past adventures. On the basis of these lexical possibilities, everything can then be said by means of allusion and plays on words. Thus the jewels can be altars, which are either much frequented, dilapidated, abandoned, well perfumed, ill-served or bored.[17] The 30 attempts to use Mangogul's ring provide a structuring model for the 30 chapters. The goal is to show the gap between appearance and reality as confessed by the ring and thereby to articulate by means of a process of lexical and semantic contamination, or by a simple play on masculine pronouns, all those loves which were either unexpected, hidden or forbidden. The ingenuity of the verbal play involved is highly amusing, but in no event does it become troubling or give rise to any desire for further pleasure. The register is flirtatious and playful, rather than erotic or obscene, and the position assigned to the reader is not as constraining as in the pornographic novel, so the process of reading brings its own satisfaction to the desire it creates. There is no need to return to the real world, since the text is entirely closed, relying on the quality of the word play and the capacity of the text to evoke without stating explicitly and to contaminate with salaciousness those words that seemed to be least amenable to such a process. There are no bodies offered up to the gaze, no embraces to be spied upon. The intrusion is entirely linguistic in nature: the parties are led to admit their loves rather than to describe any details.

For it is the body that is the key element of the erotic novel, as is underlined by so many passages from *Jacques le Fataliste*, offered up to the eye but yet also at a distance, at the same time against its will, but both complicit and reticent. A good illustration of this ambiguity can be found early on in the novel in the episode where the peasant woman carried by the doctor falls over. 'And as he was turning round to demonstrate he pushed his companion, made her lose her balance and fall to the ground, one foot caught in his coat tails, and her petticoats over her head.'[18] The text adds slightly further on, creating a sort of retrospective effect, 'after all, underneath her petticoats this peasant girl had a nice little body, as Jacques and his master had noticed. Love hasn't always waited for so seductive an opportunity.'[19] Everything about the mechanism of the erotic unveiling becomes clear: a brief glimpse of the flesh, the suggested voyeurism, and the part played by dream and desire. *Jacques le Fataliste* abounds in these sorts of descriptions: the half-naked girl who compromises Richard, Dame Suzanne sitting on the slope and exposing herself to Jacques, Justine in the half dark of the younger Bigre's attic, and perhaps best of all the description of the colour sketch that he intends to propose to the artist Fragonard:

> MASTER: . . . Describe your picture to me and be quick about it, because I am dropping with sleep.
> JACQUES: Imagine yourself in front of the Fountain of the Innocents, or near Saint-Denis' gate – two accessories which will enrich the composition.
> MASTER: I am there.
> JACQUES: Picture, in the middle of the road, a carriage with a broken spring turned over on its side.
> MASTER: I can see it.
> JACQUES: A monk and two prostitutes have got out of it. The monk is running away as fast as he can, the coachman rushing to get down from his seat. The coachman's dog has escaped from inside the coach and set off in pursuit of the monk, whom he has caught by his tails. The monk is trying everything to get rid of the dog. One of the prostitutes, dishevelled, and with her breasts showing, is splitting her sides with laughter. The other girl, who has received a bump on the forehead, is leaning against the door holding her head in her hands. Meanwhile, the populace of the town has gathered round. Street urchins run up shouting. The shopkeepers and their wives are all at their doors and other spectators are at their windows.[20]

All the elements are in place: the semi-naked body suddenly the object of indiscreet looks, those spectators who only indicate a position for the reader from which to look at the body described. And it is no matter of chance that the Master should be delegated the role of reader in this book and Jacques that of the narrator, who likes the way that pictures tell stories, but who knows nothing about colours and schools. Here is the key element of the erotic novel: the making of pictures, organized in order to solicit the gaze, a call to the reader that he should take up the proper distance from the narrative in order to see, to admire and to examine. Thus the erotic narrative is to be understood as some sort of slyly made painting, a tableau of furtive gestures, a sort of strange dark room, an intrusive perception where the models behave as if they were not seen, or, absorbed in their pleasures, behave as if there were no witness.[21] On the other hand, if there is a witness whose presence is accepted, then he will take full part in the proceedings. The mere voyeur is excluded. Or rather, he cannot belong to the erotic picture – as many examples show – unless the moment of intimacy itself is spied upon in secret. The picture is always seen through a gap, a narrow window, a secret door, a two-way mirror. This is not to say that the witness is dead to what he sees. The picture perceived by him is an invitation to take part in the festivities, to take his part of the pleasure he glimpses. This witness is the very figure by which the reader's own desire is written into the text.

The erotic novel is then in essence a novel about voyeurism. The description of the tableaux and the setting of the scene which are proper to it correspond to that primary condition. We will show what sort of rhetoric is put into practice by such an organization of the narrative. This sequence of observations will allow us to understand more easily some of the distinctions in this large corpus of literature, and perhaps some of the more important differences between the *roman libertin* and the pornographic novel. In the first of these genres there is no accumulation of embraces, no sense of furtiveness, and none of the pictorial scene-setting that we have in the pornographic novel. The *roman libertin* does not seek to engender desire but to show how a strategy of seduction is put into practice. How does one obtain the favours of a woman (and especially those that were referred to in the genre as the 'dernières faveurs') in spite of social, moral, psychological and religious prohibitions? The *roman libertin* rests essentially on the art of persuasion, for to seduce is to bring the other person to give way to the insistence of desire, and to recognize, by means of a mechanism that is not so far removed from that of religious conversion, that the one who preaches the law of pleasure is right and that one must yield to that law. It is therefore a novelistic form based on dialectic, and on the art of persuasion, in which the reader and the person who resists must both be seduced and persuaded to give themselves up. Whatever one might think of it, the *roman libertin* is therefore an intellectual and cerebral exercise, a work of words and not of pictures. From a schematic point of view, the pornographic novel takes up where the *roman libertin* finishes.

Unlike the *roman libertin*, however, the erotic novel never depicts any resistance to the act of love. There is nothing except the sight of bodies offering themselves up freely, spontaneous desires and immediate pleasures. If there is resistance, then all the better to season the depiction of a rape scene, where the victim will turn out to be a free, consenting agent who shares in the pleasures of her attackers. The notion of the obstacle, so central to the *roman libertin*, is a stranger to the erotic novel. The most one might find there are material obstacles, and those are quickly overcome. In the meantime, it is that phantasmagorical proliferation and availability of bodies, always ready and always desiring, that characterizes the erotic novel and permits the accumulation of its episodes. It would not be an exaggeration to say that the erotic novel postulates that all men and all women, of whatever age and condition, are ready to respond to the first overtures they receive. The population of the erotic novel is always in search of new bacchanalia, and it is in the nature of the genre to offer them the opportunity to experience them and to offer them to the reader.

3

The Powers of the Literary Imagination

The writing, reading and censorship of the erotic novel raise questions about how the literary imagination functions. Paradoxically, the power of censorship grows with the power of the printed word. If the censors condemn lampoons, then that is because they are convinced that such works are capable of producing civil disobedience, of inspiring a spirit of revolt and so placing the powers that be in danger. If it actively seeks out antireligious texts at the behest of the Church, then that is because it seems that these works pose a threat to the institution of faith. If licentious works are pursued in the courts, then that is because the censors are certain in their minds that such texts promote moral corruption. To follow the censor's argument, every reader of a licentious work becomes an empowered libertine. It is as if, in his mind, the work had a power to convince against which nothing could prevail. It is inherent in all censorship that there should be a very high value placed on the power of print and a corresponding devaluation of the capacity of the individual to resist the forces of subversion.

One might well wonder why the censoring authority, instead of banning works and thereby crediting the printed word with almost supernatural power, did not answer fire with fire and printed word with printed word. In fact, such measures were used: abbot Chaudon's *Dictionnaire antiphilosophique* appeared in response to Voltaire's *Dictionnaire philosophique*, and Moreau's *Les Cacouacs* in answer to Voltaire's *Contes*. The satires of the

philosophers were met by Palissot's *Les Philosophes.* It is well
known that, since the days of Richelieu, the ministry routinely
paid men of letters to write defences of the status quo. Last but
not least, we could cite the large numbers of apologies that make
up a considerable proportion of the literary production of the
period, even when compared with the numbers of *romans libertins.*
But what is there to oppose the erotic novel? It is hard to imagine
what an anti-licentious novel would have been like: perhaps those
sentimental novels with their virtuous heroes and heroines. However, anti-philosophical literature did not stop at the denunciation of the content of Enlightenment works; it adopted the same
forms, as if the impact of impious and subversive literature derived not only from its content but also from its literary form.
We know what the erotic novel owes to its style, especially in
respect of its perceived effect (the immediate passage from reading to action), and so the counter-text had to borrow its narrative
strategies. The medical treatises to which we have already referred – Tissot's *De l'onanisme,* and Bienville's *De la nymphomanie*
– use the same devices, methods of depiction and dramatization
as the erotic novel for their case studies and for the illustration
of the consequences of erotic stimulation and practices. It would
be easy to find instances of the same mechanisms of accumulation and reprise, of similarity between the visualization of symptoms in the medical treatises and the narrative strategies deployed
in the erotic novel. On a formal level, the attempt to produce an
adverse reaction directly reflects the inducements offered by the
erotic novel. Against that, one of most common defences of the
erotic novel was that the evil and its effects must be shown, as
must the redemption that its victims can hope for. The literary
attack on the erotic novel therefore found itself in an impasse.
Saturnin, the hero of *Dom Bougre, ou Le Portier des Chartreux,*
is finally struck down by the pox. Carried to Bicêtre, he faces an
operation that may save his life. 'My hand fell where the pain
was at its worst. Ah! I am no longer a man!' All that remains for
him to do is to return to the convent to find peace there. 'O my
son', said the friar that received him into the house, 'Praise God:
he keeps this port open to you after so many shipwrecks. Live

here and live here in happiness if it is possible.' A false lesson if ever there was one, and easily given the lie by the epitaph that Dom Bougre has carved on his tomb: 'Hic situs est Dom Bougre, fututus, futuit' ('Here lies Dom Bougre, who fucked and was fucked'). Such a conclusion does nothing to erase the effect of the erotic episodes of the novel itself. At an opposite pole we might situate Sade's *Les Infortunes de la vertu*: the savage attacks to which poor Sophie is subjected are simply so many ways of showing that nothing can shake her virtuous constancy.[1] By these means, Sade praises the power of virtue and the frequently impenetrable ways of Providence:

> Doubtless it is cruel to have to describe, on the one hand, a host of misfortunes overwhelming a sweet and sensitive woman who has respected virtue above all else, and, on the other, the dazzling good fortune of one who has despised it all her life. But if some good springs from these fatalities, should one feel remorse for having recorded them? Can one truly regret the writing of a book wherein the wise reader, who fruitfully studies so useful a lesson of submission to the orders of providence may grasp something of its most secret mysteries together with the salutory warning that it is often to bring us back to our duties that heaven strikes down those at our side those who have best fulfilled her commandments?[2]

The successive versions of *Les Malheurs de Justine* were to prove that Sade's project was in fact some way removed from the proclamation made in the opening pages of his work. But, without going into an examination of the work's afterlife, we must nonetheless recognize that this unexpected religious conclusion does nothing to weaken the effects of the licentious passages.

However, the plan here is not to envisage the possible responses to erotic writing, but rather to understand the representation of the imagination at work in the reading of licentious literature. The issue of the imagination is raised not only in the question of censorship, but also in the writing and the reading of the erotic text. We cannot necessarily take as read what the theoreticians and those who denounced the imagination were saying, to the point of believing the imagination as defined is present in the writing and reading of licentious texts. All we can do is make a note of the coincidences, the shared sensibilities, and be content with hypotheses which, if they explain the behaviour of the censor more than the reading process, are nonetheless at the centre of the debate on licentious literature in the eighteenth century.

We know that during the classical period the imagination did not exactly get a good press. There is a constant opposition of 'the mad woman in the attic', 'the powers of deception', to the certitudes of reason. However, from Malebranche onwards, the impulse arises to understand the functioning of the imagination rather than simply to condemn it.[3] Rather than give a full account of material that would have only a minimal importance to the present discussion, I will concentrate on a few details that illustrate how thought on the subject influenced attitudes to the erotic novel. Although the imagination is widely condemned, there nonetheless exists a current of thought that gives it some value and shows its role in the progress of the human spirit. In 1760 the marquis of Feuquières published the *Phantasiologie ou Lettres philosophiques à Madame de . . . sur la faculté imaginative*. This text attempts to show the importance of the imagination in scientific progress, even if the author does recognize that there is a side to the faculty that 'knows no other law than that of its whim and, leaping from one idea to another, falls, without forethought and entirely at the mercy of chance, into either Venus' wardrobe or the lair of Poliphemus . . .'[4] and which goes so far as to believe that 'that which is possible has as much reality as that which is real.'[5] A year before, the Baron of Holbach published *Les Plaisirs de l'imagination*, a translation of Akenside's poem in three cantos. He therein affirmed his belief that the imagination occupies a middle position between the bodily organs and the moral faculties, is attached to 'channels by which we receive some of the greatest pleasures we can experience, and that it is therefore natural that those men of an ardent and sensitive disposition and temper should seek means by which to recall and relive the delicious perceptions that those faculties provide, even independently of those objects that originally produced them.'[6] We could then follow the shifts and eddies in the relations between imagination and memory, imagination and pleasure, imagination and artistic creation, right up until Delille's poem *L'Imagination*, which dates from the very eve of the French Revolution. Let us not forget that Diderot played an essential role by means of his researches into sensibility, his willingness to understand how thought is constituted, starting from elementary sensations, and his ongoing inquiry into the effects produced by literary illusion.

Thus the imagination, so much at the centre of Enlightenment thought on human nature, is also present in the questioning and inquiry into the process of reading, whether the perspective adopted is aesthetic, medical or simply moral. Yet, even though a conception of the imagination as an inventive rather than simply an imitative and passive faculty begins to appear, from a literary point of view, there is more weight placed on the reception of the literary text than on its production. Or rather it is in the effect produced that is the measure of the qualities that went into the creation of the work. The inquiry would therefore centre on the reading rather than the production of the erotic work. The civil censor and the religious authorities only rarely wondered why and how it was that the erotic text ever came to be. When they did then the answers that they obtained were often rather simple and stereotyped: vice, desire for material profit, a will to corrupt, degeneration in taste, madness. For the main part, the reflection focuses, as is fairly natural in a repressive perspective, on how one prevents or forbids this reading.

The emphasis is then on the act of reading, but especially on the reading of novels, for the major place for inventive imagination is in the enormous production of novelistic fiction at that period. Little account is taken of poetry, and only occasionally does one see a reference to Jean-Baptiste Rousseau's *Ode à Priape*, as if people were convinced that erotic verse does not have the same incitative effect as the novel. It seems to be an accepted fact that the imagination is at work only in the reading of this fictional form. It was even argued that the novel had a value, not from an aesthetic point of view, but in terms of the depth of emotion that it inspired. 'The object of the Arts', notes Helvétius, and here he is also thinking of the novel, 'as I have already said, is to give pleasure and thus to excite in us sensations, which although not painful, are nonetheless strong and vivid.'[7] The extent and size of the strength of emotion inspired by the novel, and thus the aesthetic value of the genre, can be gauged by reactions to the publication of *La Nouvelle Héloïse*.[8] In *Mon bonnet de nuit*, Louis-Sébastien Mercier contrasts the sense of boredom and passivity he experiences in reading speeches and tragedies to the exaltation that he felt at reading Jean-Jacques Rousseau's novel:

> I opened a volume of *La Nouvelle Héloïse*, which, like all other works, is no more than ink on paper, but, all of the sudden, I nonetheless become attentive and animated, heated and enflamed. I am buffeted by a thousand different emotions. I imagine myself in the groves at Clarens. I can see and hear the characters, and I read the volume in a single sitting. And when I learn that there are six of these volumes, my heart flutters with joy and pleasure, and I wish that this reading could be infinitely prolonged.[9]

Reading novels, to believe the opinions of certain authors, produces an emotion that is physiological in nature, a sort of over-excitement that is almost pathological. Rousseau's correspondents describe in some detail their troubled state in reading *La Nouvelle Héloïse* – shortness of breath, insomnia, nervous agitation or languor – all of these being signs that the medical literature of the time condemns.[10] In that regard, the medics placed particular emphasis on the dangers for women in such reading, dangers that resulted from the qualities of their imagination – the sensibility of their fibres, soft, fluid and delicate, all of which renders them especially susceptible to the effects of reading. Tissot describes the cases of 'a woman who suffers convulsions after a few hours of reading', and of a girl of ten who 'read when she should have been running about, and who at twenty is a vapourish woman and does not nurse well.' The idea is not limited to the medical literature, but dominates treatises on the education of women and young girls.[11] Femininity, the imagination and the disturbing effects that result from the reading of novels are some of the more common subjects to be found in such literature in the second half of the eighteenth century. There are very few who oppose it.

It is also one of the stock episodes in the novels of the time. Unsavoury characters play on the sensibilities of heroines by making them read novels and thereby leading them to the most unexpected excesses. In a rather mediocre novel, but one that is nonetheless perfectly representative of the genre, *La Folle de Paris ou Les Extravagances de l'amour et de la crédulité*, published in 1787 in Paris, Nougaret depicts the worrying effects of reading. More extraordinary yet is a tale by Jean-Vincent Delacroix, in which a young girl who reads *Les Amours de Lucile et de Doligni*, overcome by her readings, gives way to the entreaties of her suitor. Delacroix shows how the seducer profits from the emotions inspired by reading. Other examples can be found in the epistolary novel: both *La Nouvelle Héloïse* and *Les Liaisons dangereuses*, the best-known representatives of the form, tell how women are seduced by the reading of letters shaped by those found in fashionable fictional works.

We could quite easily add many more examples of the effects of reading, but it would nonetheless be wrong to argue that the reading of the erotic novel was merely a particular case of a more general phenomenon. If anything, the converse is true. The reading of licentious works is, in fact, exemplary for all other forms of reading and, indeed, beyond that for all writing. One could even argue that it represents all that is not said in a reflection on writing, reading and the actual effects produced by artistic representation. The long debates about novelistic fiction, which is accused of being false and immoral, are well enough known. History is put forward in opposition to the novel (Lenglet Dufresnoy, *L'Histoire justifiée contre les romans*, 1734), as per the classical dictum that one should entertain and instruct at the same time. The novel would then be open to condemnation because it weakens the reader's grasp on reality, leading him or her to prefer the fictive dream. As we have seen, the erotic novel is attacked on slightly different grounds. Doubtless there is a process of a loss of a sense of reality in so far as it contributes to a loss of moral values, leading to excess and imprisoning the reader in the narrow realm of his passions and making him forget the wider concerns of the real world. But is it not the case that the powerful physiological need it creates leads to a return to the real? As a negation of the world of morality, the erotic novel also provides a powerful affirmation of the physical world, be it only present in the desiring body of the reader, which is focused on an attentiveness to the self and to the autarchy of pleasure.

More obviously still, the erotic novel reveals a nature masked by convention and by social and religious prejudice. In that it could be described as 'philosophical' in the sense that eighteenth-century France would have understood the term – taking philosophy as the struggle against prejudice and stifling habits of thought. Elsewhere, this irruption of the physiological into the space of reading would represent a more brutal vision, but also a more accurate one of the novel's effect on the sensibilities, and which the theoreticians of the novel cited by way of defence. It must also be conceded that the lieentious novel provides an exemplary demonstration of one of the strategies of the Enlightenment, for is it not the novel of education par excellence, bending the reader's will to that of the text? The erotic novel, far removed from the careful circumlocutions of philosophical discourse, unveiling the will to power that, from many points of view, can be seen as one of the more perverse effects of the lessons of the Enlightenment.

One might well think that this is rather a lot to be laying at the door of either the erotic novel or the Enlightenment. Let us look to the similarities and note by way of conclusion that, if the erotic novel has recourse to the pictorial to sway the reader, then it falls in line with one of Rousseau's wishes, expressed in *Emile,* that the teaching of philosophy might be founded on the imagination, and speak to the eye better than to the ear:

> In neglecting the language of signs that speak to the imagination, the most energetic of languages has been lost. The impression of the word is always weak, and one speaks to the heart far better by the eyes than through the ears. In wanting to turn everything

over to reasoning, we have reduced our precepts to words; we have made no use of our actions. Reason alone is not active. It sometimes restrains, it arouses rarely, and it has never done anything great. Always to reason is the mania of small minds. Strong souls have another language. It is with this language that one persuades and makes others act.[12]

It is very tempting to apply this statement to novelistic writing. To believe some of his readers, Rousseau himself would have put the doctrine into practice in *La Nouvelle Héloïse*. Pierre de la Roche, writing to Rousseau, reproached him for those scenes which were a little too broad and which he had exposed to the eyes of his readers, and he underlined 'the effect that such depictions can have on them'. For the sake of clarity, he adds: 'you must narrate and not depict, for it may happen that there is some woman or girl who will be unable to stop her imagination placing her in that situation, and it may be that she might really be exposed to such a situation . . . She will fall, not like, but with Julie, and it will not be the head that will lead her into evil, but rather the heart that you have spoiled by your descriptions that are all too broad and vivid . . . Everything will be forgotten except for the picture, and the imagination that will attach to it and the nature of woman will go further yet . . .'[13]

This criticism from Pierre de la Roche merits further attention. Not only because it intuitively underlines the importance of the visual in the function of the erotic text but also because it attempts to gain some insight into the reader's relation with it. It is not that there is a pure and simple assimilation to the characters ('not like, but with Julie', he writes), or of some projection of the reader into the unfolding plot, but at the opposite pole perhaps, there is some discussion of the effect, the work of the text on the reader. To put it in its crudest terms, the reader is not seized with a desire for *jouissance* because the author describes the desires of his characters, but rather because there are bodies and an embrace. As much as to say that the initial coincidence of the readers and characters lasts but a mere instant. The harmony between description and effects exists only within the premises of the narration itself. The reader remains in a state of desire even when the text uses all its resources to depict the pleasure experienced. We will return to the powerlessness of the text actually to speak the moment of orgasm, of *jouissance* itself. Thus, when the episode finishes, the effect continues through the desire to which the text has given rise and which it cannot satisfy. There is a double disparity in the temporal schemata: in both the crowning of the episode and the survival of desire beyond the text itself.

We cannot therefore speak of an identification between the reader and the characters in the erotic text. The exteriority linked to the tableau renders it impossible: no reader would want to be Saturnin, the hero of *Le Portier des Chartreux*, but he would wish, like him, to experience physical pleasure. Without doubt, he would also wish for the easy seductions that are allowed for by the licentious text, that endless availability of bodies, but this time carried over into daily life. The erotic work always returns to the realm of daily life, to the body of the reader, worked on by the text and swept away by desire, far removed from these beings of ink and paper and the fictive world they inhabit.

It is in that respect that erotic literature is an exemplar of all literature, especially the novel, where there is expressed the wish to create an illusion of reality which would be as real to the reader as reality itself (this is a historically datable conceptualization of novelistic fiction, I will admit), but which is at the same time the negation of reality, since to make the reader prefer illusion over reality, literature must accept its own abolition, making way for a return to the rather prosaic damp spot of daily life, for which it had appeared to substitute itself so successfully.

4

The Limits of
Pornographic Writing

One might well be tempted to believe that the effect produced by the pornographic text is simply a function of an accumulation of episodes of sexual activity. Therefore all that would be needed for an erotic text would be a series of embraces. This is partly true, for there can be no erotic text without a multiplication of couplings, caresses and embraces, without moments of pleasure repeated and renarrated through the course of episodes which are always different and yet basically the same. One might object here that a rather more refined eroticism, in the sense that we use the term now to distinguish it from pornography or obscenity, would be cerebral to the point of eliminating all those bodies joined together and to the point of being reduced to a mere working drawing, to a metonym or a subtle equivalence. Take, for example, the coach that carries Rodolphe and Emma Bovary off through the narrow streets of Rouen, and whose curtains hide their passionate pleasures from view. We know what is happening because we imagine it on the basis of certain quite logical and clear suggestions from the narrator, along with a few details that are vouchsafed to us: the drawn curtains, the order repeated to the coach driver to continue on his way, when tiredness and thirst force him to stop his nag. We know both by imagination and deduction, even though no tableau is offered up to us. Emma's body is absent, as is Rodophe's fiery embrace. The reader who guesses and surmises, as would a detective, on the basis of signs left to him or her is not a voyeur, and that is the main difference. One might still advance as a counter-example, to stay with Flaubert, Marie Arnoux's soft, cascading tresses in *L'Education sentimentale*. The reader guesses as fast as Frédéric Moreau that they refer to hair other than on her head, and that the description of their lustre and softness circumvents both literary prohibition and a psychological inhibition that applies to the body of the woman he loves too well. But there is nothing pornographic or obscene about this; quite the contrary: the respectful embarrassment that the text forces the reader to feel for a woman whose face is half lit by a bedside lamp, with her hairbands evoking order and discipline (unlike Rosanette's disordered locks), a scene far removed from the immediate and brutal arousal of desire found in the erotic text.

The depiction of sexual activity is therefore a key element, but perhaps not sufficient in itself. Pornography is, after all, a strategy of writing. Or rather, for the pornographic text to fulfil its function, which is to produce a desire for physical pleasure and release in the reader, then it must put into operation a writerly strategy that is capable of producing that result and that result alone. That is to say that erotic literature is univocal, produces one meaning and is hostile to any attempt at interference or blurring.

There could therefore be pornographic texts that did not measure up to this requirement and which could therefore be seen as failures, that is to say that they would not produce desire (and here, not in the sense of trouble and anxiety, but rather in the most basic physiological sense of the term) in the way that a pornographic text is supposed to do. There would be little point in taking texts too far removed from the genre for the purposes of this analysis – for example, libertine or spicy literature – but rather to show how, in those texts that employ all the narrative elements necessary to pornography, there might be some sort of subversion or interference that would compromise the pornographic effect. We will therefore discuss those sorts of problems and failures in this chapter, explaining the mechanisms at work. In other words, we will analyse the sort of disruptions and interruptions that would mean that the pornographic text would fall short of its aim, without going so far as to speak of those texts that are not purely pornographic. Not that such texts are totally devoid of interest, however, and not simply because they allow us to throw light on the modus operandi of successful pornographic works, but rather that, by their very faults, they present certain qualities of writing or moral and philosophical propositions that must be measured by a different yardstick.

On the basis of this hypothesis we could set out to establish a form of catalogue of erotic books that do not achieve what they set out to do. That is to say that it would not simply be a question of decrying them from a moral or aesthetic point of view, or denigrating them from the perspective of a taste that would oppose the erotic to the obscene, but rather ranking them according to their ability to create and impose that incitatory effect of erotic literature, which specifically defines these works as erotic in nature. Not that this project would not be tempting, and, indeed, it is its paradoxes that offer the greatest interest. The result would be a sort of inverted hit-parade, which would be entirely in keeping with the interest taken here in a literature that can be written but which it would be out of place to analyse. Nonetheless, the project would be practically impossible, and instead I will offer a study of some of the forms of interference that can affect the erotic text, leaving the joys of a more systematic inquiry into the history of those erotic works that were less than earth-shaking to others who come after.

Two preliminary remarks: most commonly, those who undertake this sort of study are dealing with hybrid works, where the wish to produce desire is not sustained. Thus it is not unusual in the pornographic episode for there to be a sort of suspensory discourse or hiatus situated, generally, at the end of the sequence. Only rarely does this function as the initial means of seduction itself – such an act being entirely unnecessary, since, as we have seen, the case is already decided: in the world of pornography, it is taken for granted that men and women desire one another. The only possible problem lies in finding the right place and the right time. This discourse is often to be found after the moment of climax, often in the form of a pause, and sometimes motivated as a moment of repose that would be necessary from a physiological point of view. The language is most often moral or philosophical in tone, which is to say that there is no break in the thematic continuity. There would be no question of passing from an erotic episode into some sort of picaresque, for example, or into some other form of episode, for this would be a relaxation of the erotic tension. So there is a passage from the construction in the form of tableaux, with the description of the various bodies and their different couplings (any dialogue between the characters at this point pertaining to desire and to the body, after a short scene-setting introduction giving some information about the plot and the heroes), to a speech pronounced by the person who initiated the sequence, a speech pertaining to questions of morality and to the legitimacy and nature of sexual pleasure. Thus, in *Dom Bougre ou Le Portier des Chartreux*, there are passages on young love, on pleasure, on the vices commonly occurring in convent life, and on how desire always stirs again, barely having been satisfied. A fifth speech deals with the perversity of monks, which is then followed by a speech in praise of 'bougrerie', one on the right to pleasure and one on the improper use of confession by monks. These interventions constitute a series of pauses or distractions, even if their importance to the plot is obvious. Nothing is superfluous, since, if these discourses are not essential to the narrative, then they provide some moral justification for the behaviour of the characters or contain anti-monastic satire whose function is to make believable and verisimilar certain episodes in the narrative. However, it is also true that such passages in the narrative also bring other strategies into play. The reader's attention is not solicited in the same way as it is in those episodes that are, properly speaking, erotic, since they are based on exhibitionism or voyeurism. The suspensory discourse either plays on some obvious intertextual relation to justify its position (criticism of the monastic life, satire on moral lapses in religious life), or presents itself as more argumentative in nature, thereby appealing to critical reflection. We know that a number of passages of philosophical writing in Sade's work are lifted word for word from the baron d'Holbach, La Mettrie or Voltaire, a proof that one is no longer in the same universe as that of the erotic passages.[1]

Although the position of the reader is central to this analysis, this key figure can seem rather unreal, and that body so often discussed can seem rather abstract. Everything appears to be played out in the relation between text and reader, but in terms of a relation where the specificity of the reader counts for very little. For there is no doubt that the desire of the reader can be born only from the work of the text, but it is also necessary that the particular affectivity of the reader, especially in so far as this translates itself on the plane of sexual desire, as well as his or her preferences, allows the writing to work on the body and mind of the reading subject. We know that the act of reading engages the reader on a variety of levels: his or her cultural memory, relation to the historical conditions of the time, and affective or biological state. In theory there would be no two identical readings within a group of readers, and no two readings that would be the same for the same reader over time. We therefore come face to face with what seems to be an insurmountable difficulty that goes with the desire to be able to reconstruct all the possible readings of a given work for a given period. Let us suppose that individuals in a given cultural community, because they participate in the same historical moment and have the same educational background, also, for a large part, read very much in the same way. Let us also posit that on this shared basis is superimposed what is particular to each individual. There again the analyst is faced with a tension, with a delicate balance between the communal and the particular. In the frame of this essay it would be difficult to determine further the exact nature of that balance.

Nonetheless some attempt must be made to construct a model of reading for the erotic work which would take some account of the reader. Let us advance a few simple propositions. We can imagine *a priori* that a particular erotic scene between a heterosexual couple would have no effect whatsoever on a reader who was exclusively gay by preference, and to construct on that basis a sort of table of incompatibilities between the practices of the reader and the sexual combinations narrated by the text. Such a line of reasoning overlooks some of the givens of the erotic text that would show the underlying misconceptions. One of the main features of the erotic novel is that it blurs any hard and fast sexual distinctions: a hero can be hetero- and homosexual at the same time. Saturnin is by turns gigolo, catamite and sodomite, the overdetermining principle being that of pleasure, and the tale shows that the end can be achieved by all sorts of different means and by many different paths. There is no exclusivity in the erotic tale, no fixed oppositions. Characters pass from one activity to another as if it were all the same thing, and indeed it is: the climax that is always attained. Tableaux are organized according to principles that would otherwise seem to be at odds with opinions on sexuality, but rather seem to play on one category, then another, so that the heroes are always polymorphous. It might well be tempting to conclude from this ambivalence, which is posited not as a model but as a simple fact of life, that there is at work some sort of discontinuity: each chooses the episodes that most suit his or her tastes, habits or fantasies. However, this would be to misrepresent the complex reality of sexualities, as well as that of the writing of the licentious text. The representation of sexual pleasure disguises for a large part the means that were deployed to arrive at that end. The end leads to the forgetting of the means, and all that remains is the desire for release, just as is the case with the heroes in their embraces. Without doubt the mechanism of erasure and acceptance is more complex than that, but this is something to which we will return. This relation of the reader confronted with a text will constitute the second preliminary remark to the process of blurring to which the erotic tale is subject.

As I have already said, the strict succession of episodes, without the suspensory presence of different discourses, whether philosophical, moral or social, is not enough for the effect of erotic reading to be produced. Of all the possibilities of blurring, the present analysis will study three in detail: metaphorical excess, ironic distance and, for want of a better term, what we will refer to as the specific excess of perversity.

The first two episodes of blurring will be taken from Mirabeau's novel *Ma conversion ou Le Libertin de qualité*, published for the first time in 1783, reprinted in 1784 and then issued a third time in 1790.[2] And, first of all, we should look at some of the blurring derived from the use of different vocabularies. One of these belongs to the most crude and basic spoken register: from the outset, there are usages such as 'vit' ('dick'), 'foutre' ('to fuck'), 'cocu' ('cuckold') and 'branler' ('wank'), as well as all the innumerable variations, as one might expect, on the word 'cul' ('arse'): 'jouer du cul' ('take advantage of someone's arse'), 'bondir du cul' ('to leap [at the sight of] an arse'), 'son jean-foutre de cul qui va comme à la grêle' ('his fucking ass that goes like nothing on earth'). A certain realism in amorous practices is present throughout *Ma conversion*: people 'wank', they have 'le vit en feu' ('the hots'), there is offered 'la molle épaisseur d'une ample fessure ('the soft fullness of an ample rear'),[3] and they exhibit 'their weapons' 'a full eight inches long, raising their lofty head into the sky'.[4] The characters even use more specialized vocabulary, known only to those who regularly frequented closed houses: 'I grasped her in my arms, and in an hour I had her sweating. The croupade, the American and Dutch wheelbarrow positions . . . by God! I swear that she was born to it. The joys of nature!'[5] There is no lack of the graphic reconstitution of narrative space, even to the point that it is totally saturated by bodies in a succession of embraces anchored in one another so that they constitute a machine for the production of sexual pleasure. There is no episode that is not devoted to bouts of amorous activity, no narrative diversions, and there are very few digressions (only on music, on the actual philosophy of the monks, and on dance). The process of interference and blurring lies solely in an excess of metaphorization. For as much as the discourse of the body is realistic and precise, not shying away from crudity, so, with the exception of the reconstruction of space, saturated with desiring bodies caught in their embraces, the vocabulary of that embrace is flawed by the excess of metaphor. On the one hand, Mirabeau dives headlong into mythology without avoiding all the ridiculousness of a culturally coded language. 'And her words died on her lips. The hour struck on Cythera; love waved its flaming brand in the air; I flew on its wings, I push on and the skies open to me ... I triumph ... O Venus! Cover us with the belt of the Graces!'[6] On the other hand, he is ready to make use of rather imprecise strings of hyperbole: '... I draw her veils aside: what treasures I find delivered up to me! Shame did not groan at my desires ... She no longer knows herself ... Swift as lightning I tear through the cloud ... And the cry that escapes her lips is the sign of my victory.'[7] Most often the hero speaks of 'crossing the threshold' and 'paying a visit', of 'the altar in front of which incense is to be burned', and is especially fond of metaphors inspired by horse-riding: he 'gets up to a gallop', he 'paces his nag', which 'sweats in harness'. It is also true that these metaphors are as often as not glossed by use of the verb *foutre* either at the outset or by way of conclusion. But the reader will recognize that the crude use of such language does not provide for any real effect:

> I like to fuck. But, as God has not wished that we should find the secret of perpetual motion, one must eventually stop, for the game tires one before it grows tedious. Now, my lady always used the same language, and, as I was no longer stoking her fire, she was nothing but a rather flat and monotonous being. How I love to see those things that a woman drunk with passion can make so precious! How the right word can raise the worth of a caress, and make it all the more touching! Take away all the preludes to pleasure, and the magical words that ecstasy brings forth and so often help one to plunge back into it again ... and tedium yawns with us at the breasts of our beautiful women. Love flees and the swarms of its pleasures flies away, and one falls asleep never to awaken.[8]

Once the introductory verb is forgotten, one might even be reading the elegant and discreet reflections of a moralist. This as as much as to say that the use of a verb is not enough in itself, for the licentious novel is precisely the narrative and lexical gloss on those verbs that are at the same time too precise and too vague, and one could furthermore define it as the infinite and highly imaged commentary, the usage and conjugation of the verb *foutre* itself.

The use of metaphor thus appears as the recourse of a writer who wishes to avoid 'the repetition of monotonous details', and who is aware of the poverty of the language pertaining to the description of matters of love. The only remaining recourse is the eroticization of further lexical material, the register being defined from the outset by the key term *foutre*, which means that the language of war, horse-riding or religion can be quite easily transposed into the language of love. On the condition that the reader remembers to apply the same process of transposition throughout the reading of the work, which seems to establish another relationship between reader and text, that is not the constraining position aimed at the production of the erotic effect, implying rather a certain withdrawal, a play, a taking of distance. Despite the crudity evident at certain moments, the register seems more loose than obscene.

This distancing in *Ma conversion* is accentuated by a will that is both explicitly signalled and put into practice, to make the erotic less realistic by an accumulation of word-play. This process begins with onomastic practices in the work: heroines bear names which are often something other than patronymic in nature. There is 'Madame Honesta', an honest woman, a procurer called 'Madame Saint-Just', as well as those ladies from high society whose interests are reflected in their titles: 'Madame la baronne de Conbaille' ('Gapecunt'), 'Madame de Culsouple' ('Madame Tightarse'), 'Madame de Fortendiable, and the hero's older mistress 'Madame In aeternum', as well as a younger woman, rather more oddly provided, named 'Madame Vitauconas' ('Willy-in-the-cunt'), who will be succeeded by 'Madame Culgratulos' (whose maidservant is called 'Branlinos', a name that plays on the verb *branler*, 'to masturbate'). It would be hard to recognize in these names any particular pretence towards realism. At most they raise a smile, but their subtlety is not such that the reader might wonder about their hidden meaning. Such vague jokes only have the effect of interfering with the effect that the erotic text is trying to achieve.

Naming practices in *Ma conversion* participate in the general ironic play of the text, an irony that is essentially expressed through

plays on words and through literary quotations used in very odd
contexts. The word-play is sometimes incredibly poor, involving
such words as 'bidet', although it becomes more subtle, whatever
one might think, when it starts to incorporate the prefix *con-*.
Thus, to a woman who invites him to seduce another by that
same means, the hero replies: 'Ah! Madame, you know how I
push it; as a witness . . . (you can feel the gesture I made). She
took me at my word, and the witness found himself in a *confrontation*.'[9] Or even more subtle: a bishop recounts how the countess of Minandon, apparently prudish, infected him six months
previously, and the hero replies, 'That is what happens, monsignor,
when you leave your diocese (*condom*) . . .' The commentary in
brackets and the transcription in italics prove that one cannot do
without the sort of distancing effect created by the play on words
that would refuse the constraints and the univocity of the erotic
text per se.

Let us add to that that the frequent use of quotations out of
context, or more precisely in a context that is not their own. In
a bout of love, the hero encounters an obstacle that dismays him,
and the text notes '*the flood that brought me to that shore ebbed
in alarm*'.[10] If he is subjected to a practice that he did not expect,
and which reverses sexual roles: '*Would Rodrigue have believed
it*? And, as for me, . . . *Would Chimène have said it*?'[11] The
quotations – extracts from theatrical works, love poetry, bawdy
songs or even clerical language are plentiful and have a parodic
value. They force the reader into recognizing the parodied text,
the italics being the most obvious invitation to decode what is
being said and to appreciate the wit and the humour that lie
behind it. This is a procedure that clearly has little to do with the
strategies of the erotic text, and moreover we must be quite
specific about the sort of reservations that are being expressed:
there is no question of denying the possibility of humour, irony
or word-play in literary texts, or even to deduce from that that
the analysis and the analyst are not able to appreciate the function of an unexpected quotation. If they are thought to be out of
place, then this is in relation to a schematic, functional view of
the erotic text which forms the basis of our approach. From that

point of view, these references form a sort of diversion orienting the reader towards a reading that is not strictly that of the erotic text. It is obvious that everything that incites the reader not to take the text seriously distances his reading from the effects the licentious text is thought to produce. To speak ironically, or to raise a smile, compromises the close relation to the text that, ideally, the reader should have. Pornographic literature requires a strict focus: therein lies the contract and condition of its effectiveness, from both a textual and an extratextual point of view. Thus the licentious work is the refusal of any compromise or adulteration whatsoever, for how can one consider as incitatory a novel that depicts the gymnastics of love in the following manner?

> One day, when we had done, l'faith, all the follies the Aretine depicts in his most religious work, did it not happen that the marquise took a fancy to my posterior. The joke and the compliment that I had made to her little man made this idea all the stronger, and she wished, by all the strength that she could muster, to execute her design . . . Have you ever seen a parrot defend its tail from a sly and crafty little cat? There I was, jumping like a fish, twisting and letting off strings of farts, but the she-devil was not to be shaken off . . . I can feel it still . . . ouch!'[12]

In the light of such passages, one might well wonder if parody were not the main feature of *Ma conversion*. It is not only the quotations that reveal this, but also the entire collection of metaphorical excesses, which are presented and used to parody a variety of discourses, such as that of gallantry, heroic literature and the language of the Church. Since parody supposes a reading on two registers, it is fundamentally opposed to erotic writing, which is always strictly conditioned and self-sufficient. There can be no parody in the erotic except of the erotic itself, which is then the negation of parody. From that point of view, the parody of the bucolic novel undertaken by Mirabeau when the hero of *Ma conversion* decides to abandon Paris, with all its works and its pomp, represents a strategic break in the process of writing, and as a consequence in the effect derived from the reading of the different episodes:

You are familiar with those enchanted palaces that overlook the tranquil course of the Seine ... Alas! A cruel art pursues us yet, stifling nature when it thinks to beautify it. The tedious symmetry has framed these terraces with sterile sand and these sad lawns bare of all greenery. It is not walls of hedgerow that allow zephyrs to caress Flora's breast. The rose withers without honour in these vases that restrict its growth so as to group it into a bunch with others of its kind.[13]

One might concede that the reader in quest of heady sensations might well be disappointed by such a style. Why not argue therefore that Mirabeau is playing with the reader in much the same way as Diderot did in *Jacques le Fataliste* and seeking to undermine his expectations? We would not go as far as to state that the tension thus created mirrors that of the unsatisfied reader.

The heroes of the licentious novel have, in general, a quite remarkable aptitude for pleasure. They are creatures of desire, always ready, spared the contingencies and limits that physiology normally imposes. The chaste, the continent and the impotent are excluded from their company. Their behaviour tends to prove that the desire is present in everyone, as a potential that only requires the right occasion – and indeed sometimes demands it – to show itself with ardour and violence. It is doubtless for that reason that the prude and the devotee of religion occupy only the occasional paragraph. The serenity of the convent is simply an appearance: monasteries and convents form the favourite backdrop for the most depraved practices and scenes of complete disorder. There is a sort of demonstrative necessity inherent in such sexualization. There is no age and no estate that does not find itself caught up in the elaborately choreographed saraband of sexual activity. Virgins, both male and female, are necessary heroes in this movement towards a certain demonstrative saturation, as, logically, are the old and the deformed. The erotic novel thereby oscillates between a hymn to the beauty of the perfect body, and the depiction of other bodies, or even the same ones, in states of decrepitude, deformity and disease, between the aesthetic and the pathological – not that this ever forms an obstacle to the all-devouring pursuit of physical pleasure. *Ma conversion* confirms this logic of the erotic tale. We find juxtaposed the charms of some of the partners with the following portrait of Madame In aeternum:

> Imagine, my friend, a vile child of some sixty years. Her face is an inverted oval, with a wig that has cleverly been worked in among the remains of her hair, dyed, of course, and the fastening carefully disguised. Her red eyes squint so that she looks as if she is forever glancing somewhere off to the side, and an enormous mouth.[14]

This is not the only such picture. The hero later satisfies an old nun, whose principal charm is that she has lost all her teeth. 'I lay her down on her bed and had sweet commerce with her twice (as many times as she still had teeth) ... "May the Good Lord thank you for what you have done". She said, much moved. I laughed and noticed a little stump that still remained at the back of her mouth.'[15] He also struggles with a giant woman in an almost titanic erotic duel: 'Imagine a colossus of about five feet six inches in height, whose black, wiry hair covered a low forehead, with two large eyebrows that lent her eyes an even more terrifying aspect, and a vast mouth. A sort of moustache sits under her nose which is covered with Spanish tobacco. Her arms, feet and hands are all those of a man, and her voice I initially took to be that of her husband.'[16] One might object that the attraction of a body that is either worn out or monstrous might be more in the realm of common fantasies, and that the strategy of the erotic text has nothing to do with that, but rather more with the pursuit of pleasure and *jouissance*. The excitatory effect does not work by identification but rather by parallel: the reader does not want to experience the same pleasure as the hero, but rather to experience pleasure at the same time as the hero experiences his. This proposition holds true to the point that the scene of his climax with Madame In aeternum is one of the most striking descriptions to be found in the novel. Thus ugliness and monstrosity do not interfere, but there is an element of the grotesque:

> May the devil take me if her convulsions did not hold me in the sweet bliss of illusion a full five minutes. The old devil came as if she were a woman of thirty, and it took her a long time to recover from it, being exhausted, emptied. As for me, I was in a fine sweat . . . But here is another story. As I was wiping myself down, I found a double wig, which was that of my old harlot, which was only lightly stuck on, and had therefore joined with mine out of fellow feeling. The old woman was in a laughable state of disorder, with her bonnet and the rug that did service for hair, everything had gone to the devil . . . she looked absolutely disgraceful.[17]

The grotesque elements are pushed so far with the old nun that the hero even attempts to pull out the stumps of her teeth without succeeding. As for the Herculean American woman, she catches a cold in the course of her pleasures and dies horribly of a chest infection. Even if it is true that in an erotic text the important thing is to move from one episode to another, so that there can be a change of partner and so that the pleasures of the text can be continued, we must nonetheless recognize that the transition is scarcely verisimilar, and shows a rather relaxed attitude to the reader. Even then, he would have to be attentive to these narrative elements.

There is a third sort of interference which is extremely complex, and of which many examples can be found in the works of the Marquis de Sade, and especially in *Les Cent-vingt journées de Sodome*. Sade's works show absolutely meticulous organization from an erotic point of view: a succession of episodes given over entirely to intense physical pleasure, the most effective use of lexical effects by means of the eroticization of other vocabularies, the disruptions and shifts of meaning, use of rather crude technical terms, tableau-construction, all with that formula so often used by Sade's characters: 'let us now take up our positions in the pose'. There is nothing lacking from the paraphernalia of the erotic text, and yet there is no doubt that Sade's novels are not pornographic. Why such a restriction of the genre? It is quite common for people to spring to Sade's defence when the charge of pornography is levelled, indeed of a pornography that is especially degrading for the spectator. The reader will have understood that it was not the intention of this essay to contrast pornography – in the sense of low-quality literature falling outside the bounds of correct taste – with the sort of eroticism that seems to have some quasi-metaphysical value, any more than it would have been a question of defending pornography from the judgements that are generally formulated against it. As far as we are concerned the genre is simply of interest as a laboratory study of literature at work. Whether pornography is an art form has little importance. What is important is to understand by means of its maniacal and captivating writing the exemplary way in which writing can have an effect on the real world. For, and it cannot be repeated enough, the reader of the pornographic novel is subject to a constraint that most authors can only dream of imposing. To read a pornographic novel and to be subject to its influence is perhaps in some way to experience something of the essence of literature. Consequently, there is no question of condemning Sade any more than one should praise him for having failed to write the perfect pornographic text. Rather the debate is on another level, the real issue being how it is that sadian pornography stops or falls short. This is not a question of morality or the hierarchy of genres, but more of the interference and blurring at work that prevents the consummation of a particular process that has already been set in motion.

Should one recall at this point that the heroes of Sade's novels are more talkative than desiring? Rather more than physical pleasure it is the justification of the means that they use to attain that end. A discourse of some sort generally forms the prelude to the moment of pleasure, and it often happens that the speech has some excitatory function. This is, obviously, contrary to the implicit narrative of the erotic text, for the body has its reasons, for which the speech sets the scene by creating the interval, the pause between the acts. First pleasure and then speech, the time to explain matters to some innocent but benighted young man or woman who is nonetheless well disposed, and to catch one's breath and to begin the pursuit of pleasure once again. Yet the speech is merely a pause since the hearer is already won over, liberated from his or her prejudices and scruples. And yet the speeches in the pornographic novel function rather more as excursuses, suspending the narrative and distracting the reader. The introduction of such material makes the reader abandon the world of desire to be introduced into the world of understanding and reflection. There is nothing more here that pertains to the world of the erotic tableau, or to the sort of distance required by the voyeur. All these features are accentuated and carried to their very limits by the sadian narrative, which wishes to be the bearer not of sexual excitation, but of truth. The didactic tendencies which characterize Sade's prose assigns to the reader a position that is not that of desire. He does not experience the desire to act like the characters in the novel; at the very most he can give way to the arguments advanced and recognize their persuasive force. Nor will he feel driven to pass from reading to the act, no more than he would feel driven to take the stage and pontificate. The philosophical material does not constrain the reader, rather it obeys other strategies and manipulates him or her in other ways. Let us note last of all that the philosophizing in the pornographic novel not only interferes during that discourse itself, but, more generally, it subverts the entire teleology of the erotic work which then becomes heterogeneous. The fact is so obvious that pornographic novels almost inevitably deconstruct themselves, eliminating those philosophical remarks that are thought to be superfluous or incongruous, or which would disturb a reading that was based on the desire for physical pleasure. What person who was familiar with the ways of the *Enfer* has not received the advice from some reader to let the book fall open by itself on the desk, which is without doubt the best way to read the best pages!

The sadian novel presents another sort of interference which is specific to it alone: the interference by means of the introduction into its episodes of philosophical passages that are only an exaggeration (sometimes a monstrous one) of the sort of narrative practice that was sketched out in *Thérèse philosophe* or *Dom Bougre* itself. It is more a question of the erotic model that is put to work in the sadian narrative, and which strongly contradicts the sort of aesthetic and imaginary of desire on which the pornographic novel is based. We know that the fascination that it exerts on the reader stems in a large part from the infinite resources of desire in the characters. For some of them, the novelistic space is one of revelation. Thus it is not rare for the adolescent hero (and the same holds true for the heroine) to discover, by a half-glimpsed embrace, the reality of his (or her) sexual appetites. The pornographic novel only exists by means of that mad dance of bodies looking for one another. The shameful, the impotent and those who abstain are not converted to sexual pleasure, but rather are resolutely cast out into the novelistic void. The pornographic novel constitutes itself from that point of view as a community of pleasure. The virgin is taken by surprise, although once her fear has passed she enters into the space of pleasure. Likewise, the experience of sodomy, a common enough practice in the erotic novel, evokes pain as a transitory state, a prelude through which it is necessary to pass in order to attain orgasm. There is nothing of the sort in Sade's work. Here, pleasure is something rather solitary, and the other is only a means to that end, an object through which *jouissance* is attained, and not a subject experiencing pleasure in his or her own right. The other suffers and sometimes tries to defend him- or herself, but most often submits passively to the power of the master. *Jouissance* is the privilege of the aristocratic classes. In the closed château of *Les Cent-vingt journées de Sodome*, torturers fulfil their desires and their victims die as a result of it, slaves are sacrificed and suffer without drawing any sort of pleasure from it. With the exception of Justine, the sadian novel presents us with very few masochistic heroes. Its universe is more that of violence than of pleasure. Without doubt, one might argue that the means do not matter and only the end is important, which is often true of the pornographic novel. However, the sadian novel presents such differences in narrative strategy that the comparison becomes meaningless. The invitation to pleasure is bound up with perception, with the setting and with the pleasure experienced by the heroes. Hence the necessity for a writing structured in the form of tableaux, a concept which I will discuss in more detail in a later chapter. Now, if we follow Sade, one of the most important devices for scene-setting is that the suffering should be perceived by the person who inflicts it and who will themselves arrive at orgasm by so doing. This act of *jouissance* in the sadian novel is more proffered and described by the person who experiences it than by an observer, providing an image for the reader's own consumption. The difference is considerable, since this discursive quality sabotages the production of desire in the novel. Let us add last of all that the tableaux presented are not generally intended as sensual. Blows, mutilation and the insistent recourse to coprophagy are not means apt to give rise to desire. The very excess of the sadian description may reveal the infinite spaces of the human mind, but nonetheless it distances the reader from the text and prevents the sort of suspension of disbelief that is central to the novel's effect on the reader. We thereby pass from the excess of desire which is used to give rise to the desire for *jouissance* by means of its very enormity to a world of excess where the extremes of pleasure dwell alongside monstrosity and death.

5

Clandestine Literature and the Art of Self-Designation

From the documents giving details of seizures, from the archives of printers and booksellers, from private correspondence and from autobiographical and fictional accounts taken from Chevrier, Rousseau or Rétif de la Bretonne we can reconstruct more or less how books that were licentious, banned and pursued by the inspectors of the book trade circulated and were bought. We know from a variety of sources the importance of hawking and all the possible variations on that theme – 'the seller woman in the toilet', who carries 'piquant' works, suggestive pictures and messages with the fancy gew-gaws that she sells. Then there is the figure of Célestine, who becomes a bookseller in order to help her love life.

The expressions that go with this trade are well known: 'livres de second rayon' (a term that covers not only the private bookshop but also the shop known to the book trade or the hawker's basket, and thereby passes from a material localization to a moral or social plane), or 'vendre sous le manteau', or even the literal equivalent of our English expression 'to sell under the counter'. All these expressions point to one fact: the banned book, whether pornographic or not – for what matters here is its illicit character – never appears in public. The risk would be too great. One is therefore reduced to choosing it on the basis of its reputation or according to other more specific criteria, all of which mean it has quite different characteristics to those of other books.

Thus materialist works of the eighteenth century are often advertised by their titles alone. D'Holbach's *Le Christianisme dévoilé* or *Le Traité des trois imposteurs* and *Les Nouvelles libertés de penser* clearly indicate the nature of their content for those who are familiar with the main themes of libertine thought. For a member of philosophical circles the expression 'bon sens' speaks volumes, and can even function as a highly coded title to the work of the curé Meslier, a priest and notorious atheist, and to that of d'Holbach. *L'Homme-machine* by La Mettrie also takes on considerable significance because of the way it echoes Descartes' writings on the animal-machine and by a combination of terms that would have been mutually exclusive in the idealist tradition.

Because it is for purchase in a greedy, semi-clandestine setting, by a public of connoisseurs and others used to the rules of the game, regular and faithful clients of the hawker, the erotic novel must identify itself from the outset according to a particular code, quite different from that of the novel whose title obeys its own laws and which can be subtitled either 'récit' or 'roman', or even 'mémoires authentiques'. For the banned book in general and the pornographic novel in particular is not the sort of thing that one can flick through at leisure, and of which one might read a page or two before going on to buy it. It is not a book for display, but rather one that is seized in a sudden and furtive manner. Sometimes the seller will give a few details, and Rousseau reminds us that the woman who lent out novels in Geneva during his adolescence attempted to incite some interest in him by means of a language appropriate to his age, founded on a sort of fearful attraction to sexual matters ('to emphasize their value, she used to name them to me with an air of mystery . . .'). Mercier, in *Le Tableau de Paris*, gives some impression of the sort of sales tactics practised by the hawkers in the arcades of the Palais Royal or along the rue Saint-Jacques. Chevrier's *Le Colporteur* offers a paean to the art of persuasion practised by these sellers, who were themselves most frequently without any education and often as not completely illiterate, and we know from police reports how successful they were at getting into the antechambers and the salons in order to ply their trade. Such a strategy is not always possible, even with all the skills of the mountebank and the cleverest of ploys to whet the appetite. Rather the book must announce what it is from the very first furtive glance, inviting the reader to buy and to read, making itself something that people would desire to read, and thereby paving the way for another desire.

We must therefore recognize that there are techniques working by means of the title, the illustration and the overall presentation. These techniques can be, and were, codified, and they were very effective. Moreover, they were indispensable, whatever the means of approach that was put into practice. On the one hand, they might be useful to confirm the estimation of the salesman, who will always be suspected of partiality – it is worth noting that the lending woman in Rousseau's account should have failed because she probably tried rather too hard, and thus failed to convince her prospective client. On the other hand, they precede it: almost won over by the opinion offered by the salesman, the client seeks some confirmation by means of a rapid flick through the work, beginning with the title.

Title Pages

Whether it belongs to a banned or a licit book, the title page gives an important message. It decomposes into a series of elements: the title itself, whether accompanied by a gloss which can be constructed in a variety of different ways, then the name of the author and then, at the bottom of the page, the place where the book was produced, the name of the publisher and the date. In addition to these three elements, the only really indispensable one of which is the title, there is sometimes another indication about the presence or absence of illustrations ('accompagné de figures' or 'avec figures') and some sort of epigraph or exergue, whether in the form of verses or a quotation in Latin or some other phrase unattributed to any author. There is generally some sort of vignette between the exergue or the title and the name of the place in which the book was printed. More rarely the title page is decorated with an ornate frame, which can be picked up again in the bar separating the place of publication from the name of the press and the date of publication. Without going into too many details, let us note furthermore that the title page, and it is the only page in the book to do so, uses different typographical characters for different elements of its make-up. It can also happen, but this is rather more rare, that the title page has as a sort of facing page an engraving which can, by means of a caption, refer the reader to a particular passage in the text, or which can be of a more general character, giving some sort of pictorial suggestion as to the nature of what is about to be read.

If it is obvious that all these elements have a meaning, either by their presence or their absence, then the sense that is produced and received by the reader results from their combination. It is not unusual for the same sort of typographical characters to be used for two elements, or two parts of different elements can be the sign of a connection that the reader is invited to draw. The title page is therefore a very complex device. The only differences between a banned book and one that is permitted lie in the fact that the former has to say very quickly, and often with a considerable degree of emphasis, to exactly which register of prohibited literature it belongs, and that the work does not designate itself by means of a clear and simple category, such as 'pornographic book' or whatever, as one might sometimes put a description such as 'a tragedy' or 'a novel' or, even, 'a prohibited book'. If pornography is subject to constraints imposed by the rapidity of the transaction, it is also subject to those of periphrasis, for it must speak clearly and yet allusively – a balance not easily struck. Nonetheless, the mechanisms at work do permit of some codification, and we will attempt to reconstruct some part of that system here.

Two preliminary remarks first of all: the object of the inquiry is to find out what message the title page of the licentious work sends to the customer who looks it over. Can its message actually be limited to a simple designation, 'I am a pornographic novel', without some value judgement also intervening so that the desire to read can be made all the more pressing: not merely pornographic but also of the best of that genre, giving the impression that one might know what 'better' meant? Does it not also allow pause for reflection on how the title page gives to understand about the nature and quality of the work that it announces? Should it not offer some sort of implicit demonstration and furnish some sort of proof, making its lines speak more then they appear to do? Since the reader is not yet embarked on the quest for the particular effect of erotic literature, but rather in a sort of prelude that is rather less strictly defined and whose role is to produce the desire for desire, which, for want of a better word, one might refer to as curiosity, then parody and a few flashes of wit might not be out of place in the same way that they would be in the body of the text itself. They participate in the seduction that is the function of the erotic novel. Let us note last of all that all this demonstration does not apply to those erotic works that are well known, and which already belong to a cannon of erotic literature. The purchaser of *Dom Bougre* in the 1780s knew what he was dealing with, and so the techniques deployed in the title pages of later editions do not have the same function, or even any real function at all; at most, their role is merely supplementary, and constitutes something more of a confirmation. The purchaser has not bought the wrong book.

In the world of titles the reader must be able to distinguish the canonical titles from the later imitations and continuations that might seek to profit from the established reputation of a particular work, and which might be confirmed by a simple complicitous allusion. Note first of all that, among the more canonical titles, some of them (although this is rather rare) offer very little foothold for analysis. There is nothing or very little in them that announces their content, as is the case with *Le Diable dupé par les femmes*, described as a 'nouvelle critique et galante par le Sieur F. N. Henry, sur l'imprimerie de Paris, chez la veuve Dubreuil, quai de la Tournelle, à l'image de Saint-Georges', which seems to be a piece of apocrypha, and whose connotations tend to refer the reader more to medieval farce than to an erotic work of some sort. More surprising still, the first edition of Mirabeau's novel is entitled '*Ma conversion* by M. D. R. C. D. M. F., published in London in 1783'. One could be forgiven for thinking from the title page that the text was that of a work of piety. In all events, the title of the second edition shows a significant change: *Le Libertin de qualité ou Confidences d'un prisonnier au château de Vincennes, écrites par lui-même.* Confirmation of the erotic character of the text it contains is given by the indication of the place of printing: 'Istanbul, the Odalisque Press'. In the 1783 edition it is only the presence of engravings, announced on the title page, and which would be rather rare in a work of piety, that gives any hint as to the exact nature of the text at hand. The place of publication given in the 1783 edition could also be rather a surprise, since it would be rather hard to imagine a Catholic work of piety published in a Protestant country. For a reader from the end of the eighteenth century it is clear that the place of publication is fictive, something rather strange for an edifying work which would not appear to require such a subterfuge. Sometimes also the title can be written in something of the neutral tone generally reserved for historical works, such as *Monuments de la vie privée des Douze Césars, d'après une suite de pierres gravées sous leur règne*, published in Caprées, at the house of Sabellius, 1680, a text that was reprinted several times during the century, and of which only the word 'privée' in the title might attract the reader's attention. The sequel reveals something of the real nature of this text: *Monuments du culte secret des Dames romaines, pour servir de suite aux Monuments de la vie privée des Douze Césars . . .* (1784). In the 1787 edition, the place of publication is changed to the Vatican Press. It is difficult to take account of the titles that are given away by either the epigraph or the fleuron – as is the case with Mirabeau's *Le Rideau levé ou L'Education de Laure*, whose erotic connotations are rather tenuous. The image of the raised curtain evokes the theatre as much as the revelation of a secret, and the second half – *L'Education de Laure* – seems to refer to the novel of 'initiation', a genre that was beginning to emerge. However, everything is explained by the epigraph: 'Back with you, . . . Censors; / Flee, devotees, hypocrites and fools; / Prudes, ugly old trouts, and you old shrews; / Our sweet transports were not written for you.' The illustration represents a couple embracing surrounded by a border of leaves, and, to complete the overall effect, the place of publication is given as 'Cythera', all of which amply suffices to modify the impression of apparent neutrality of the double title.

There is another series of canonical titles, this time rather more explicit. These can be classed more or less strictly. First of all there are those that are organized around the terms *galant* and *galanteries*. We will go from the most neutral, *L'Année galante ou Etrenne à l'Amour, Contes enrichis de Figures et d'Ariettes* (1773), to the more brutal *Histoire galante des deux maquerelles les plus célèbres de la capitale des Welches,* published in Cupidopolis in 1785. A more moderate example is *La Belle Allemande ou Les Galanteries de Thérèse*, published in 1740, not to mention a title that does not beat around the bush, *Les Amours, galanteries ou Passe-temps des actrices ou Confessions curieuses et galantes de ces dames, rédigées par une bayadère de l'Opéra,* published in 'Couillopolis' in 1700, with, as an epigraph: '"To achieve pleasure is all." Actress' maxim'. We will note that the term *galanteries* ('love affair/intrigue') is more expressive than the adjective *galant*, and that the virtually anodyne quality of the latter is sometimes compensated for by the content of the second half of the title, by the place of publication – 'maquerelle', 'Couillopolis' – or by means of the epigraph. Certain terms or certain places: 'l'Opéra', 'les actrices' or 'une bayadère' ('dancing girl'), all of which had strong connotations at the time, also had the function of marking a title that might have had little impact. If this type of title operates by circumlocutions and veiled allusions, as in the case of *La Belle Allemande ou les Galanteries de Thérèse*, it also knows how to call a spade a spade and to use very brutal and crude terminology – hence the *Histoire galante des deux maquerelles* . . .

A second group is organized around the term *amour(s)*. There are a good number of titles constructed around the formula 'Les Amours de . . .', such as *Les Amours du Saint-Père, soi-disant Pape, avec Madame Victoire, ci-devant dame de France, ou Conférences infernales, libertines et sacerdotales, entre le Pape, les rois de Coeur, Trèfle, Carreau et de Pique, leurs concubines . . .,* which is a pamphlet from the revolutionary period, or *Amours, galanteries, intrigues, Ruses et crimes des capucins et des religieuses depuis les temps les plus reculés jusqu'à nos jours* (1788), or again the famous *Les Amours de Charlot et Toinette, pièce dérobée à Voltaire,* a politico-pornographic pamphlet targeted at the royal couple, and published for the first time in 1779. Crude anti-clericalism or relatively transparent allusions to current events mark the work out as erotic. It is rare that the term *amours* allows for anything more subtle. In his reply to Sade's *Justine,* Rétif de la Bretonne tried to do something of the sort in writing *L'Anti-Justine, ou Les Délices de l'Amour,* but this is then caught up in a nexus of indicators that is rather more effective than the simple term *amours.*

Within the same lexical field of love, of gallantry and of its effects, another body of titles is based around the terms *libertin* and *libertinage.* Some of these titles are realist in nature, such as *Correspondance d'Eulalie ou Tableau du Libertinage à Paris, avec la vie de plusieurs filles célèbres de ce siècle* (London, Jean Nourse), with the epigraph to the effect that 'Paris is one of those immense cities where there are a good number of wealthy, de-bauched people concerned only to buy for themselves all sorts of disgraceful pleasures, and which poverty is quite happy to provide.' Others refer back to a well-known tradition, such as Mirabeau's *Le Libertin de qualité,* already discussed, or again the rather later *Monrose ou Le Libertin par fatalité,* published in 1792, with the epigraph 'O Venus! Mars owed you greater pleas-ure'.[1] One might also quote *Le Parnasse libertin, ou Recueil de poésies libres* (1769), which, in its first edition, seems to have been published by the booksellers Cazals and Ferrand at Amster-dam, and which, to give a clearer indication of its content, is given in the second edition as having been published by le Dru ('vigorous/lusty'), at the sign of Priapus, in 'Paillardisiropolis' (a pun on *paillard,* 'lewd', and *désir,* 'desire') in 1772 (this work went through about ten editions). More clear still is the title given by J. B. Nougaret, *Les Progrès du libertinage, historiette trouvée dans le portefeuille d'un carme réformé. Publié par un novice du même ordre.* This work is decorated with engravings, and emanates from the printing press of the abbess of Mont

Martre. Note that the message is absolutely unequivocal for this group of texts: the word *libertin* is quite transparent for eighteenth century readers.

Taking these lexical elements as a point of departure, it is quite simple to construct the groups that derive from them, depending on whether they opt for a very crude and direct gloss on the terms *amour* and *galant* or whether they rely on some sort of metonymic derivation. Among the first group we might number *L'Art de foutre en quarante manières ou La Science pratique des filles du monde*, published in Amsterdam in 1789, or a rather more refined work, *L'Art priapique, parodie des deux premiers chants de l'art poétique par un octogénaire* (1764), or even *Le Cabinet d'Amour et de Vénus* (Cologne, Pierre Marteau & Sons). One night finally note *La Courtisane anaphrodite ou La Pucelle libertine* (Avignon, 1787). The gamut runs from the most discreet, such as *Les Egarements de Julie* (London, 1776), to the most daring of all, which must without doubt be *La Foutromanie, poème lubrique en six chants* (1780). It would be difficult to be any clearer. As for the derivations, these pertain to what one might term the props and the places commonly found in erotic literature. We might begin by citing Fougeret de Montbron's *Le Canapé couleur de feu* (with its variant, *Le Divan*, by Grébillon fils) or, rather more crude, all the pornographic literature of the Revolution, based on the theme of the *godemiché* ('dildo'), such as *Le Godemiché royal* (1789), or *Le Godemiché royal, suivi de Mea culpa et de La Garce en pleurs et Les Derniers soupirs de la Garce en pleurs*. In this group we can also classify all the titles pertaining to the brothel, which are very common during the revolutionary period, such as in the case of *Le Bordel national sous les auspices de la reine, à l'usage des Confédérés provinciaux, à Cythère et dans tous les bordels de Paris* (1790), or *Les Bordels de Paris, avec les noms* . . . published in year II of the revolutionary calendar, 14 July 1790, or *Les Bordels de Thalil ou Les Forces d'Hercule* (published in st Petersburg, at the house of 'compère Mathieu'). In more refined literature, the *locus amoenus* becomes the boudoir, which then evokes the intimacy of a society setting – as in the case of *Les Passe-temps du boudoir, ou Recueil nouveau des contes en vers* (published in Galipoli, at the house of the widow Turban, the bookseller on the 'rue de Ramasan' in 1787) and, of course, *La Philosophie dans le boudoir* by the marquis de Sade, or *Les Offrandes à Priape ou Les Boudoirs des grisettes, contes nouveaux et gaillards*, published in 'Conculis' in 1794. Among this last group of titles there are a number that use traditional and fashionable literary forms, which are then simply eroticized by the context. Thus, *L'Ode à Priape* by Piron, *L'Ode aux Bougres* (1794), *Les Heures de Paphos, contes moraux, par un sacrificateur de Vénus* (1737) or *Les Etrennes aux fouteurs ou Le Calendrier des deux sexes*, published in both Cythera and Sodom. And most likely to be found in the pockets of those who condemned the genre in 1793, *Les Etrennes gaillards, dédiées à ma commère, recueil nouveau de contes en vers, de chansons et d'épigrammes, etc.* (1782). Again, we might well add to this list the various *Arts: L'Art de foutre, L'Art priapique*, or those revolving around the term *cabinet* ('closet/small room'), such as *Le Cabinet d'Amour et Vénus* (published in Cologne, by Pierre Marteau & Sons) or *Le Cabinet de Lamysaque ou Choix d'épigrammes érotiques des plus célèbres poètes français*. Another term that was used was the *cadran* ('hours') – *Le Cadran de la volupté ou Les Aventures de Chérubin* – or even the catechism, as in the case of *Le Catéchisme libertin à l'usage des filles de joie, et des jeunes demoiselles qui se décident d'embrasser cette profession* (1791). Again, we might well cite the example of the various 'correspondences', such as *La Correspondance d'Eulalie ou Tableau du Libertinage de Paris, avec la vie de plusieurs filles célèbres de ce siècle*, or *La Correspondance de madame Gourdan, dite la Comtesse, avec un recueil des chansons à l'usage des soupeurs de chez madame Gourdan* (London, 1784). Another recurrent motif is that of *les délices* ('the joys'), found in titles such as *Les Délices de Coblentz ou Anecdotes libertines des émigrés françois* (Koblenz, 1792) and *Les Délices du cloître ou La Nonne éclairée.* (1761), or of mock eulogies such as *L'Eloge des tétons, ouvrage curieux, galant et badin, composé pour les divertissements des dames* (Cologne, 1775), or conversations, as in *Les Entretiens de la grille on Le Moine au parloir* (1693). There are a great number of variations on the term *histoire*, where the erotic charge can lie either in a reference to some well-known scandal (*Histoire du Pére Jean-Baptiste Girard, jésuite et recteur du collège de la Marine à Toulon et de la demoiselle M. C. Cadière*), and which was used in the famous *Thérèse philosophe ou Mémoires pour servir à l'Histoire du P. Dirrag, et de mademoiselle Eradice*, or in the use of the adjective *galant*, or rather less ambiguous terms such as *maquerelle* ('procurer') or *godemiché*. There is a similar play on the term 'letters', so much in fashion among the novelists of the second half of the eighteenth century. We therefore have *Lettres galantes et philosophiques des deux nonnes, publiées par un apôtre du libertinage*, with the following comment by way of an epigraph from Petronius: 'It is not a crime to portray the tender feelings Nature inspires in us.'[2]

From this collection of titles, showing the various means used by the erotic text to designate itself, we can begin to discern some of the organizing principles. Note first of all that they proceed by opposition: a neutral title is supplemented by a crude commentary or some place of publication which reveals the disingenuousness of the title. As much as to say that none of the elements of the title page can be taken in isolation. From the title, they proceed by a progressive revelation through the epigraph, the commentary, the publisher and the place of publication. The allusions involved can be very direct or carefully encoded, but in all events transparent to those familiar with the conventions of such literature. The overall effect of the different elements of the title page can even be to accentuate the more salacious ones to the point of saturation, which in itself is doubtless something that would appear very promising to the potential purchaser. To consider a larger body of the titles which were published over the period of more than a century, it would seem that the events of the Revolution accentuated the unbridled crudeness of the titles: the absence of censorship perhaps led to a period of very fierce competition, in order to persuade a reader who could quite easily chose another work. Lewd titles are very numerous, and are often imbued with some sort of clerical connotation, either naming monks and nuns as the principal heroes of their tales, or indicating that the cloister

or the convent appear as propitious places for the worst debauchery. In a corpus of over 200 titles, taken from the catalogue
L'Enfer de la Bibliothèque nationale, the references to clerics are
more numerous than those to prostitution, prostitutes or other
more conventional places of debauchery. The Revolution gave
new impetus to that tendency, with its attacks on figures such as
abbot Maury or the non-juring priests. One could well wonder
about the functioning of such an active network of images and
associations that has linked monks, priests and debauchery since
the Middle Ages and which was reactivated by the anti-clericalism
of the Enlightenment, with its criticisms of the religious life. What
is important here is that the presence of clerical elements in the
title should constitute some sort of guarantee, confirming that
what the reader has in his hand is in fact a licentious work,
playing the forbidden game of mingling the religious and the
sexual. Such titles send out a signal to the reader, sometimes
without any hesitation or pudor – as in the case of *Les Religieuses
en chemise*, which is a variant on *Vénus dans le cloître* – that
they promise the pleasure that goes with a double or even triple
transgression.

    The presence of a woman's name in the title can also serve to
designate the text as erotic. Such names are rarely used without
some other qualification, such as *La Belle Allemande ou Thérèse
philosophe*, or being connected with some sort of degrading profession (*Margot la ravaudeuse* by Fougeret de Montbron, for
example), or by some more specifically erotic reference, such as
Les Egarements de Julie, or *Felicia ou Mes fredaines* by Nerciat.
The names most commonly used are Julie, Justine and Thérèse.
The marquis de Sade will of course be the principal heir to this
onomastic tradition. What is the value of these names and what
sort of codification lies behind their usage? It seems that these
particular names, widely attested in a large sample of titles, also
have a role in the way in which the erotic text designates itself,
although it is apparent as well that the name alone does not
suffice – in which case we would have to think of *La Vie de
Marianne* by Marivaux, or *Julie ou La Nouvelle Héloïse* by Jean-
Jacques Rousseau. The name generally needs to be supported by

some other element, such as the second half of the title, an epigraph, or a place of publication or name of a printer that has some suggestive value.

Let us note last of all that the erotic novel, by its very nature, excludes all forms of humour, as if irony, by the very act of creating a distance between reader and text, could interfere with the novel's effect. Nonetheless there is a place for humour in the title. This humour is essentially parodic in nature, and the reader will recognize the reuse of titles in the works that have already been mentioned: 'lettres', 'correspondance' and other delights that are transformed by a context that is crudely and brutally sexualized. It is often the unexpectedness of the combinations that creates the comic effect, and crudity is very rarely absent. The crude is linked with neutral language and even with the language of nobility in *Le Godemiché royal* (1789) or in *Les Fouteries chantantes* or *Les Récréations priapiques* (1792). Some works even offer their own commentary on the language of mythology, as in *Les Travaux d'Hercules ou La Rocambole de la fouterie* (1790). It is not uncommon that the title should make derisive use of the conventions elsewhere deployed by the novel of the time to gain credibility, as is the case with *Antonin ou Le Fils du capucin par un religieux de l'ordre*, where the sort of guarantee offered is easily understood. Nonetheless, comic invention is carried to its highest peaks by the ingenuity that went into the various invented names of the publishers and the places of publication, as we will see.

Variations on a Theme

Certain titles enjoyed a considerable success, and there inevitably appeared a host of variations and imitations based on them. Thus we have *L'Arétin français, par un membre de l'Académie des Dames* (London, 1787), or again *L'Histoire et vie de l'Arétin, ou Les Entretiens de Magdalon et de Julie* (1774) or *Le Petit-neveu de l'Arétin, ouvrage posthume, trouvé dans le portefeuille de son grand' oncle* (1800). We will give no account here of all the many translations, where the titles are too explicit, as in the case of *La Putain errante ou Dialogue de Madeleine et Julie*, an exact translation of *La puttana errante, overo dialogo di Madalena e Giulia*, attributed to Aretino, which seems to date from the middle of the eighteenth century and which was rather oddly reprinted in 1791 under the title of *La Putain errante ou Dialogue de Madeleine et de Julie, fidèlement traduit de l'italien en françois par Pierre Arétino*, 'a new and revised edition, corrected and expanded, and with engravings supplied thanks to the generosity of Mademoiselle Théroigne de Méricourt, President of the Club du Palais-Royal, and *chargée des plaisirs* to the Left of our august Senate (1791)'. This edition unites a variety of devices for attracting the reader's attention: the guarantee provided by the name of Pietro Aretino, the well-known title, which is easily recognized, and the word 'putain' for those unfamiliar with the conventions. Last of all, there is the erotico-political reference to the name Théroigne de Méricourt.

Alongside other authors who owe their canonical status to their antiquity, a considerable corpus of pornographic literature accrued as the Enlightenment progressed, with a few titles that themselves became canonical and referential and whose titles, cited whole or in part, became part of the system that guaranteed a work's place in the ranks of pornographic texts. Such is the case of the edition of *L'Histoire de Dom Bougre, portier des Chartreux, écrite par lui-même*, with illustrations, published in Rome by 'Philotanus', almost certainly for the first time in 1740 and attributed to Gervaise de la Touche. This work enjoyed an astounding success, and was reprinted throughout the century, sometimes with amusing variations on the title. Thus, in 1777, there appeared *L'Histoire de Dom B . . . , portier des Chartreux, écrite par lui-même*, 'new edition, revised and corrected under the direction of the Holy Father in Rome, at the expense of the Chartrians'. Or again, an undated edition, this time titled *Le Portier des Chartreux*, published in Grenoble by the Grande-Chartreuse press, with the false title of *Histoire de Gouberdom* (an anagram of Dom Bougre). It is obvious that the editions are designed to entertain, since the text is already known as an erotic work and classified as such, and thus possesses in itself a sufficient saturation of information. Deriving from this, a number of eighteenth-century works use the canonical term 'portier' ('doorkeeper') in the title to designate themselves as pornographic. Examples of this can be found in *L'Histoire de Marguerite, fille de Suzon, nièce de Dom Bougre, suivi de la Cauchoise*, published in Paris at the Louvre in 1784, and which was preceded by *Les Mémoires de Suzon, soeur de Dom Bougre, portier des Chartreux, écrits par elle-même* (London, 1778). During the Revolution, Dom Bougre was pressed into service again with the work *L'Abbé Maury au bordel . . . ou Dom Bougre aux Etats généraux ou Doléances de Dom Bougre du Portier des Chartreux par l'auteur de la Foutromanie* and *Le Nouveau Dom Bougre à l'Assemblée nationale*. This is an extreme case and shows how *Dom Bougre* imposed itself as a model by dint of its overwhelming success.

The case of the novel penned by the marquis of Argens, *Thérèse philosophe*, is rather different. When the novel appeared, under the title *Thérèse philosophe ou Mémoires pour servir à l'histoire du P. Dirrag et de Mademoiselle Eradice*, undated and with the place of publication given rather dryly and simply as 'la Haye', there was little to point it out as an erotic novel except for the reference to an earlier text, *La Belle Allemande ou Les Galanteries de Thérèse* (1740), and by the epithet *philosophe*, which means a person free of prejudices, but yet more still by the daring allusion to the almost contemporary scandal of the relations between father Girard and his penitent Mlle Cadière, which had already formed the subject of a banned publication, *L'Histoire du père Jean-Baptiste Girard, jésuite et recteur du collège de la Marine à Toulon et de la demoiselle M. C. Cadière*, divided up into thirty-two plates, and for which there is no date or place of publication given. *Thérèse philosophe* was one of the great successes of the century: edition followed edition as seizure followed seizure. Sometimes the title is reduced to *Thérèse philosophe*, proof that the allusion to the scandal had lost some of its pertinence, and that the erotic elements enjoyed a certain autonomy, owing nothing more to events that were only distantly remembered or either entirely forgotten. Sometimes *L'Histoire de Madame Bois-Laurier* is given in the same volume. However, there was no direct sequel to the work, no more than there were any stories said to deal with a sister, niece or any other female relative of the heroine. Only one title refers directly to *Thérèse philosophe*, but then in an erotico-political perspective, and that is *L'Apparition de Thérèse-philosophe à Saint-Cloud ou Le Triomphe de la volupté à Saint-Cloud*, a work whose manuscript was supposedly stolen from the pocket of an aristocrat by M. Barnave (Saint-Cloud, Mère des Grâces). And yet *Thérèse philosophe* imposes a model of a title formed, on the basis of the sequence that we have already discussed, of the female first name in combination with a qualifying epithet. This formula grew very common from the 1750s, which perhaps implies that there might be some sort of formal overdetermination instead of any question of content.

Les Infortunes de la vertu, which Sade kept in manuscript form, and which Apollinaire eventually published at the beginning of the twentieth century, formed the basis for another group of derivations and related works. Thus, in 1791, there appeared Sade's *Justine ou Les Infortunes de la vertu*, whose title refers more to the *roman noir* or to the moral tale than to erotic literature. This title corresponds fairly exactly to the sort of ambiguities that operate at an erotic level in the text, whose descriptions are rather reserved and not especially suggestive. In 1797 there was a slight modification to the title, giving *La Nouvelle Justine ou Les Malheurs de la vertu*, but this is an entirely new text. Comparing the two titles reveals how the process of recall and differentiation operates, but there is nothing in this new title that announces the dark eroticism of the marquis' tale. Instead, there is a different logic, which Sade promulgated in his essay *Idée sur les romans*, advocating the recourse to any means in order to provoke terror and pity in the reader. The project is both moral and philosophical in nature, as the title of the sequel, *Juliette ou Les Prospérités du vice* (1797), proved. This went on to form a pairing with the earlier work, and they were thenceforth known under the title of *Justine ou Les Malheurs de la vertu suivi de L'Histoire de Juliette ou Les Prospérités du vice*. Sade's marginal position in the production of erotic literature at this time does not prevent us from inquiring into the effects of filiation and reprise that can be found in the various sequels to his work. Indeed, this argument is supported by the fact that Rétif de la Bretonne, the defender par excellence of healthy sensual pleasures, replied to the *Nouvelle Justine* in his *Anti-Justine ou Les Délices de l'amour*, which appeared in 1798. In both the foreword and the preface, Rétif explains his relation to Sade's work:

> Nobody was more outraged than I by the foul works of the infamous Dsds, that is to say, *Justine, Aline, Le Boudoir, La Théorie du libertinage,* . . . My goal is to create a more pleasant book than any of his, which wives can have read to their husbands so that they might be better served by them, and where libertinage will have nothing cruel to visit upon the Fair Sex, giving it life rather than bringing death, and where love, brought back to the realm of nature, and freed from scruples and prejudice, will only offer up images of happiness and voluptuousness. (preface)

The foreword is clearer yet:

> Long since sated with women, *La Justine* came into my hands. I was set on fire by the work. I desired pleasure, and it was almost with fury that I bit the breasts of my mount, twisting and pinching her flesh and her arms . . . Ashamed of the excesses that resulted from my reading, I created myself an *Erotikon* that would be gentle and savoury, but not cruel . . .

Here, then, is an excellent example of the double connection to Sade on the one hand and to Mirabeau on the other, and which shows us the process of rewriting. The foreword clearly explains the limits of the erotic effect and the ambiguities of a writing that, while trying to present itself as the refusal of a model, can only exist by means of a relation to that which it claims to denounce.

It therefore seems that the titles that are built on echoes, either in terms of form or content, or by means of the links drawn explicitly between texts, constitute an important means of self-designation for the pornographic novel. Such a strategy relies, quite obviously, on a complicity of knowledge and a shared memory. It reveals that literature has an archaeology and a pantheon. Apart from the humoristic effect of certain references, it can also appear to translate some sort of attempt to claim legitimacy. To that end, a number of titles refer to classical traditions, such as *L'Art priapique, parodie des deux premiers chants de l'Art poétique,* or Piron's *Ode à Priape,* or *Les Offrandes à Priape* (1794). Others refer to Venus or Hercules, which can be glossed immediately as salacious or obscene: *Vénus dans le cloître ou La Religieuse en chemise* (1746), *Vénus en rut ou Vie d'une célèbre libertine* (1791) and *Les Travaux d'Hercule ou La Rocambole de la fouterie* (1790). The title can also make use of cultivated language, which can even verge on the pedantic, this again being a means to advertise the erotic content of the work. Mirabeau's *Erotika Biblion* (1783), *Anadria ou confessions de mademoiselle Sapho, contenant les détails de sa réception dans le secte anandrine . . .* (1789) and *Les Aphrodites ou Fragmens thalipriapiques pour servir à l'histoire du plaisir* (1793) are all examples of this strategy. It is not unusual for the licentious work to attempt to give itself a severe and erudite veneer, as in the case of *Les Monuments de la vie privée des douze Césars d'après une suite de pierres gravées sous leur règne.* It would be wrong to see the classical character of these tales as an attempt to dissimulate the erotic character of their content, for the pornographic has no shame of itself, obeying a logic of exhibitionism that is part of its very nature, and which provides a further illustration of the strategies of self-designation, some of which we have already discussed. Any printed matter that is produced furtively and in a clandestine manner must mark itself out rapidly and unequivocally, by means of a variety of different codes, showing the genre to which it belongs and the nature of its content – all the more so for the reason that it is immoral, and the perusal of such volumes and the frequenting of those who sell them constitutes in itself a transgression of moral, social and religious norms. In fact, through these titles, which are at the same time both explicit and highly coded, is played out one of the paradoxical parts of the relationship to the erotic text. It should offer, by its own way, the awareness of a sort of break, which can be cultural as in the present case, juxtaposing the reference to classical literature and the most crude language. The use of a high register can offer some form of initiation, since the erotic text is the friend of secrecy and wishes to be seen as elitist and the property of a minority, in the same manner as those places given over to the pleasures of the senses which the novel never ceases to describe. The reference to classical literature thereby forms a sort of pass-word.

If we return to the titles that use the names of women, then it will be noticed by the same token that one can pass from the most vulgar gloss to the most subtle, as if these titles oscillated between the depths of frivolity and vacuity, on the one hand, to the most refined act of decoding, on the other. The same hesitations and shifts operate in the erotic narrative itself, as the tale passes from one sort of embrace to another. On the one hand there are the rather unsubtle titles such as *Caroline et Saint Hilaire ou Les Putains du Palais-Royal* (1796) and on the other the rather more discreet *Félicia ou Mes fredaines*, where the possessive pronoun says it all, providing for a radical modification in perspective. Between these two poles, all shades and degrees are possible: from Margot to Julie.

The corpus of canonical titles classified according to the lexical series of terms divided up into the domains of love, sexuality and the clerical can be thought of differently according to the different links that can be traced between them and their ancestors such as *Dom Bougre ou Le Portier des Chartreux* or *Thérèse philosophe*. The system is then organized by initial titles rather than by the recurrence and reuse of terms such as *galant* or *amours*. One must concede nonetheless that the significant proliferation of titles participates in the two systems: there is the use of words that have some value as a point of reference, and then the practice of derived titles that echo those of the canon. The intersection of the two systems allows the erotic text to multiply and combine the means by which it can designate itself.

There is a group of titles which present a rather more mysterious case, and which are entirely marginal to the models and types that I have discussed up until now. The indications that they give of belonging to a particular genre are so allusive that they seem to contradict the general theory. One can link Fougeret de Montbron's *Le Canapé couleur de feu* (1741) back to *Le Sopha* by Crébillon fils (1740), thereby recognizing that the sofa has an evocative power similar to that of the mention of the boudoir, while admitting that the way in which these texts designate themselves is rather less crude than in the case of the more direct titles. To a reader who was either inattentive or unfamiliar with the conventions of the genre, a title such as *L'Eloge historique de Milord Contenant* might appear to have little significance. Mirabeau's *Hic-et-Hec ou L'Elève des R. P. jésuites d'Avignon* seems rather unexpected even for someone who is aware of the rather ambiguous nature of the designation, where the only apparent erotic significance is provided by the various anti-clerical tales against the Jesuits, their odd ways and the lessons they gave. As for this last title, the second edition found itself obliged to be rather more precise: *Hic-et-Hec, ou L'Art de varier les plaisirs de l'amour et de la volupté, enseigné par les R. P. jésuites à leurs élèves.* As much as to say that those titles that were a little too chary in the information that they gave out, or too subtle in their plays on erotic connotation, required some later commentary, either by means of a gloss or by the addition of elements that would provide a clearer designation, such as the epigraph, the vignette, the printer or the place of publication.

Once again we should perhaps remind the reader of the impossibility of separating out the different elements of the title page. As we have already stated, the outlining of the relations between these elements serves to unveil, either by clarification or by saturation, the individual elements then providing an excess of information to counterbalance the gaps and reticences of the title. The complementary groups then serve to adumbrate what is not said in the title itself. Of course, the converse can often be true: there are novels where the epigraph, the place of publication and the printer seem to be entirely serious and so provide humorous contrast with a title that is clearly readable as erotic. There is one heading whose importance and role is rather reduced, and that is the name of the author. In our corpus, only one work in twenty makes any sort of reference to an author, and these cases are almost inevitably highly fantastical in any event. There are some references made in the anti-clerical tradition, as in *Antonin ou Le Fils du Capucin, par un religieux de l'ordre* (1801), or in terms of some relation to another canonical erotic work, where the author might be given either as 'la Muse libertine' or 'l'auteur du Bordel national'. The name of the supposed author sometimes serves to guarantee the licentious quality of the work, as in *Le Degré des âges du plaisir ou Jouissances voluptueuses de deux personnes de sexes différents aux différents époques de la vie*, collected from reliable memoirs by Mirabeau, 'friend to pleasures'. The same effect is to be found in *Les Heures de Paphos, contes moraux*, whose author is given as a 'worshipper of Venus'. Even though it might be rather dangerous to establish a rule on the basis of so few attestations, it would seem that the use of the name of an author, always fictive and often having some sort of referential value, functions as a guarantee of the erotic qualities of the work.

THE EPIGRAPHS

Among the large group of epigraphs, and one title in four has one, we must divide the titles in Latin (almost half) from the ones in French. A rather unrepresentative exception is the case of one in Italian taken from Tasso. Those in Latin generally come from Persius, Martial, Ovid or Virgil.[3] There are a small number that seem to come from non-literary sources. The reference to the erotic works of Catullus and Martial, or to Ovid's *Amores*, work by suggesting links, as we have already seen, without there being any particular need to look for the attempt to gain some sort of cultural cachet by means of a reference to classical literature. There is no doubt that the effect of interference produced by the Latin, by the presence of a language of high culture in a text that is often rather crude, is part of the positional ambiguity of the erotic text in the reading process. The epigraphs in French serve rather more immediate ends. A number of them are parodic:

exhortations to virtue contradicted by the accompanying title. Thus we have *L'Art priapique, parodie des deux premiers chants de l'Art poétique, par un octogénaire*, which has as its epigraph 'I have lived and I wish to be of use to those who have lived', taken from Duclos' *Considérations sur les moeurs de ce siècle*. The French epigraph, like that in Latin, may or may not refer to an erotic author. One might well find Boileau with his famous saying 'J'appelle un chat, un chat', along with Racine's equally well-known 'Venus with all her might is on her prey' from *Phèdre* (Act I, scene iii), or the Chevalier Florian: 'Predilections are part of nature and the best are those that one already has.' Some exergues are so famous as to scarcely require mention, as in the famous 'La mère en proscrira la lecture à sa fille' from *La Nouvelle Héloïse*. Note that these literary epigraphs often illustrate the crudest of titles, as is the case with the line from Racine, which in turn takes on a new significance in *Vénus en rut ou Vie d'une célèbre libertine*, as does Florian's in *Les Enfants de Sodome à l'Assemblée nationale, ou Députés de l'ordre de la manchette* (1790), Rousseau's in *Les Fureurs utérines de Marie-Antoinette, femme de Louis XVI* (1791), or Duclos' in *L'Art priapique* and Boileau's in *L'Arétin françois* (1787) – all of these works join their titles in a complex relation to their epigraph that either supports them or provides an ironic contrast. Either the epigraph offers the promise of a seductive realism, as in the case of Boileau, or it announces a work so shocking that it should be forbidden to sections of society (Rousseau), or again the work parodies the traditional moral appended to the traditional novel. Such epigraphs can in no way serve to hide or guarantee the erotic content of the works in question. They have already given some indication of that by the titles, and so the reader knows what he is dealing with. Rather, the effect is to produce a sort of amused complicity, an extra thrill offered by an epigraph that plays with literary modes of expression, and thereby offers the spectacle of an intertextual order founded on dissonance.

A second group is made up of epigraphs that refer to the corpus of erotic literature itself. Piron is often quoted, with the line from *L'Ode à Priape*: 'O Priapus, give me breath enough for my task', or in the form of an obscene reference ('All joy lies in the cunt, / but outside the cunt there is no salvation'). These quotations can then also provide a link to other canonical works in the corpus, as in the case of *L'Histoire galante de la Tourière des Carmélites*, which is described as a work 'composed to form a companion to *Le Portier des Chartreux*'. These titles show a strategy akin to that of the links and echoes that we have already discussed. A revolutionary pamphlet that we have already seen makes use of a double reference: the title, *Dom Bougre à l'Assemblée nationale*, links it to *Le Portier des Chartreux*, but the author also identifies himself as the author of *Le Bordel national*. In addition, the epigraph seems to play on this double link: 'I, Bougre, although in orders, / love wine and women. / Thus come, behold me / To fuck and to drink is all my trade.' It is obvious that the majority of epigraphs are extremely crude, and that this provides some support to the effect of the title itself. The overall effect is one of a guarantee of the work's licentious qualities and a perversion of the schemes by which the contemporary novel sought to establish some credibility. Yet while the mechanism is the same, the product is radically different.

A third ensemble is made up of those epigraphs which are apparently anonymous, and which by research have been found to have belonged possibly to a corpus of traditional erotic literature. All genres are represented here. The epigraph can contain some sort of social comment, linking in with a title that is parodic in itself,[4] or it can seem to offer some vague moral finality ('Gold triumphs over the cruellest, / This metal enslaves Venus, / And ever does blind Phitis / Reduce beautiful women to servitude'). Sometimes the epigraph has some sort of explanatory value, which can function as a promise of things to come 'The fault is with the gods who have made me so mad', for *Félicia ou Mes fredaines*, or again in parody of the many pedagogical and moral novels of the period ('A work most useful to all those young persons who wish to embark on a course of debauchery', for *La Messaline française ou Les Nuits de la Duch . . . de Pol . . .* (pamphlet, 1789). These epigraphs can also be obscene. 'Gods enter from the rear, while to enter the cunt is the act of a mere man' is the proclamation to be found on opening *Les Derniers Soupirs de la garce en pleurs, adressés à la ci-devant noblesse, et dédiée à la triste, sèche et délaissée* ... (1790). It would be difficult to establish any rigorous model that would account for the relation between title and epigraph, and there is no systematic logic that can be said to govern the relation. However, there are two dominant categories, which tend to confirm the hypotheses that were advanced for the titles and their attendant commentaries. The epigraphs have the function of clarifying and making less obscure the parodic nature of the titles, or sometimes to accent the point of them, and thereby create a sort of excess, or yet again brutally to underline the licentious aspects of the title. From these examples, it should be apparent that the epigraph plays an important part in the flexible system of signals put out by the title page.

PLACE OF PUBLICATION AND PRINTERS

The place of publication and the name of the printer form the third element of the title page, and constitute an important part of the message by which the book seeks to attract the reader. In the majority of cases they form a coherent whole, either presenting themselves as serious, or revealing an obscene inventiveness in one another. This inventiveness can even apply to the date. In the first category we could take as a model *L'Arétin françois, par un membre de l'Académie des Dames* (London, 1787). Here it is as if the title was entirely clear and self-sufficient as an index. This hypothesis is confirmed by the date and place of publication ascribed to *L'Art de foutre en quarante manières, ou La Science pratique des filles du monde* (Amsterdam, 1789), as well as that given for *Le Cabinet d'Amour et de Vénus* (Cologne, Pierre Marteau & Sons), or last of all for *La Courtisane anaphrodite ou La Pucelle libertine* (Avignon, 1787). Certain designations of printer and place of publication are rather more difficult to interpret, even though they are undoubtedly completely neutral, such as *Thémidore*, published 'at the expense of the Company, 1745', and where the epigraph, taken from Ovid, as well as the particular connotations of the name given in the title, could well signal to the attentive reader that the work at hand was erotic. The same procedure works for Fougeret de Montbron's *Le Canapé couleur de feu* (Amsterdam, The Company of Booksellers, 1741), where the vocabulary of the boudoir and the temperament implied by the colour of the sofa speak quiet volumes. Thus, in some cases the techniques deployed by the erotic novel are highly insidious and, in contrast to the general rule, function by means of discreet allusions.

What was to be understood from the title and the place of publication in a banned work was quite removed from the practices of those writings that enjoyed greater tolerance, even though names and places such as 'Pierre Marteau' or 'Amsterdam' might well suggest the contraband trade in banned literature operating between Europe and France. Too clear an indication of the publisher and the place of publication could indicate by itself that the work in question was banned, and that the indications given are essentially a false address. After the end of censorship, such addresses could serve to indicate that the work kept to the rather louche traditions of pornographic writing under the Ancien Régime. Thus, *Lucette ou Le Progrès du libertinage* (London, the Strand, published by Jean Nourse, 1765) or *Les Délassements secrets ou Les Parties fines de plusieurs députés de l'Assemblée nationale* (London, the printing press of Saint James's Palace, 1790) or, again, *L'Histoire de Marguerite, fille de Suzon, nièce de Dom Bougre* . . . (Paris, the Louvre, 1784). One must admit, as has already been noted, that if the abolition of censorship by the Revolution produced any change in the status of erotic literature by accentuating the crude exaggerations and the mixture of the obscene and the political, the weight of the traditions of a highly codified genre nonetheless retained their central importance to the point of taking the conventional signals into a context that no longer required them.

Without daring to be explicit, the erotic literature produced under the Ancien Régime, and no doubt much of the underground literature of the time, developed a series of very clear signals that had the function of indicating its true nature, even if the title had already told the reader everything they needed to know. Formulae such as 'Constantinople' or 'from the Vatican Press'[5] add more information. The anti-clerical note is not absent from these imaginary places: 'the Paraclete',[6] 'Luxuropolis, the Clergy Press',[7] 'Rome, Press of the Holy Father', or 'Rome, at the expense of the heads of the Carmelite order'.[8] Often they played on the contrast with the obscenity of the title itself. Paradoxically, the furthest place, and the most inimical to the religious beliefs of Catholic France, plays the same role as the false hint of orthodoxy. The flexibility of the various strategies put into play is remarkable. I have already discussed the links between anti-clerical satire and erotic writing, and this bears repeating here. There is quite obviously a historical dimension, the reflection of contemporary opinion and of a specific historical situation. Moreover, the denunciation of the immorality and perversity of convent and monastic life can be seen as a reaction against the attempts of the Church, in collaboration with the secular powers, to control the sexual practices of those living at the time of the Ancien Régime. Other reasons can be found to account for this particular thematic constellation: the closed society of the convent, dedicated to a life of sensuality, can be used quite easily as a figure of the self-contained economy of the pornographic imaginary, and of the writing practice by which it is encoded and represented. Let us also recall the renewed impetus that was given to the anti-clerical tradition of the Middle Ages by its encounter with the anti-religious thought of the Enlightenment.

One large group of places of publication uses place names from Greece or from classical literature, in themselves a clear signal to the aficionado of pornographic literature: 'Paphos',[9] 'Cythera',[10] 'Cupidopolis', and other variations on the theme, such as 'Florence at the House of Cupidon' or 'published in New Cytheropolis'.[11] Such references are so much a part of the tradition that it is enough to say that a work is printed 'in Greece'.[12] There are several works which give as their place of publication the city of Lampsaque, in Asia Minor, on the Hellespont, famous for its marvellous gardens, fine wines and temples. Underlying all these references is the myth of Greece as the land of love, even deviant love, par excellence. This taste reflects more general trends in the culture of the day. The eighteenth century was fascinated with the figure of Sappho and with Socratic ideas of love, to which Voltaire devotes an article in the *Dictionnaire philosophique*.

But it is in the obscene nature of the places of publication and the names of printers that the pornographic novel gives its clearest indications. There is no ambiguity whatsoever, and the nature of the text is clearly designated. This obscenity serves to give an edge to a place of publication that might perhaps be a little too elegant: 'Cythera, in every brothel in Paris',[13] or 'Paris, Foutromanie Press'.[14] Some designations, although not crude, refer to the pornographic nature of the work, such as 'Luxuropolis, The Clergy Press',[15] 'Rome, Philotanus Press'.[16] Others function in parallel to the titles or epigraphs, as is the case with 'Rome, at the House of Dom Bougre, Three Virgins Press'.[17] But such moderation is the exception rather than the rule, and generally speaking the references are much cruder. Many places of publication are entirely unequivocal: 'Couillopolis',[18] 'Helion Foutropolis',[19] 'Branlinos',[20] 'Enculons',[21] 'Gamahuchons'.[22] Nor do printers and booksellers yield anything to them in obscenity: '[Crispinaille Press]',[23] 'All the whores in the Palais-Royal and especially the nuns of Montmartre',[24] 'Clitoris Press, rue du Sperme, opposite the Fountain of the Seed of the Golden Rod'.[25] One exceptional case exceeds all the others in its crudeness, and even brutality, untrammelled by any consideration of literary quality whatsoever: 'Foutropolis, at the House of Braquemart ['weapon', 'penis'] the bookseller, Tug-Dick ['Tire-vit'] Street, at the Sign of the Golden Bollocks, with the permission of the Fathers Superior'.[26]

Just as the events of the Revolution accentuated the tendency towards obscenity in the titles of erotic works, so the same process affected the places of publication and the names of the printers, mixing the pornographic with the political. One pamphlet gives 'Democratis Press, at the expense of the Demagogic Fuckers, 1792',[27] another, to which we have already referred, gives at the bottom of the title page: 'At Gamahuchon, which is found in the house of all national Fuckery, in the second year of fucktative regeneration'.[28] Another gives its date of publication as 'year One of joyous fuckery' (1790)[29] and yet another as 'in the Second Year of the dream of Liberty'.[30]

It is rare that the name of the publisher or the place of publication should be governed by anything other than this obscene inventiveness. Nonetheless, it is worth citing the case of Alphonse, known as 'The Impotent', 'Origénie, at the House of Jean-Who-Can't, The Great Eunuch, 1740',[31] or that of *L'Art priapique, parodie des deux premiers chants de l'Art poétique de Boileau,* whose place of publication was given as 'Namur, at the sign of Gulled Boileau in 1764'.[32] Last of all, there is the edition of Rétif de la Bretonne's *L'Anti-Justine ou Les Délices de l'amour,* 'published at the Palais-Royal, at the House of the late widow Girouard, most well known in the Biblical sense, and who was sometimes afflicted by a gash whose history has been "recunted", and which gave her her knowledge of erotic matters'.[33]

The position of the grouping formed by the place of publication and the name of the printer in the overall composition of the title page does nothing to contradict the effect produced by the title or the epigraph, tending rather to accentuate them. The use of crudeness and explicit language is clearly much more frequent. With the exception of a few rare cases where the elements in question are rather neutral in tone, it would appear that the last of the groupings on the title page is generally intended to be the one that removes any trace of ambiguity or doubt (just in case there were any left) in the mind of the reader as to the nature of the text.

FRONTISPIECES

It remains only to examine the frontispieces. These are rare, since not all erotic works are illustrated, the proportion being about two in three, of which only a small number have a frontispiece that interacts with the title in any way. In this section I would like to discuss four of these, *Vénus dans le cloître ou La Religieuse en chemise*, a new edition supplemented with engraved figures (Düsseldorf, at the house of H. V. Roussen, Commis des Postes, 1746 (see figure 5.1); *Les Mémoires de Suzon, soeur de D. B. portier des Chartreux, écrits par elle-même, où l'on a joint La Perle des plans économiques ou La Chimère raisonnable* (London, 1778 see figure 5.2); *Ma conversion ou Le Libertin de qualité* (1783 see figure 5.3) and *Le Décret des sens sanctionnés par la volupté*, a new work, published in Rome 'at the press of the Holy Father in 1793' (see figure 5.4). Such a small sample makes it difficult to draw anything other than the most provisional conclusions. It should be noted that the quality of the illustrations in erotic literature of this period is generally very poor, and the drawing themselves are often as not extremely clumsy and poorly executed, with errors of perspective and the most basic failures to render proportion correctly. Contrast and lighting are primitive, with a basic distribution of light and shade. Overall, the work appears that of the most rank amateur, far removed from the quality of work associated with Gravelot or Eisen, and more often given to jobbing workmen – as we can tell of the records of engravers arrested and taken to the Bastille for such offences for this period. There are no well-known names there. Not that all the engravings were the botched work of middling artists: it is known that some of the more skilled engravers often produced erotic engravings of considerable quality. It has even been argued that certain renowned artists, and this has even been suspected of the virtuous Greuze, were not above supplying really rather daring works to those who had the resources to indulge their tastes.

Thus the frontispieces in question are therefore almost all of very low quality, with the exception of *Les Mémoires de Suzon*, which is more or less acceptable, although no more remarkable than the others for its humour and invention, as we will show. Note also that the frontispiece picks up only the essential elements of the title, and that sometimes this written part is not free of errors: *Les Mémoires de Suzon* becomes *Mémoires de Suzon . . . écrit par elle-même*. The frontispiece of *Ma conversion* does without the commentary, but includes the Latin epigraph. (The very vulgar frontispiece to *Thérèse philosophe* does not take

Figure 5.1 *Frontispiece from* Vénus dans le cloître, ou La Religieuse en chemise, *Düsseldorf, 1746 (reproduced by kind permission of the Bibliothèque Nationale, Paris)*

Figure 5.2 *Frontispiece from* Mémoire de Suzon, sœur de Dom Bougre, *London, 1778 (reproduced by kind permission of the Bibliothèque Nationale, Paris)*

Figure 5.3 *Frontispiece from* Ma conversion ou Le Libertin de qualité, *1783 (reproduced by kind permission of the Bibliothèque Nationale, Paris)*

Figure 5.4 *Frontispiece from* Décrets des sens, sanctionnés par la volupté, *Rome, 1793 (reproduced by kind permission of the Bibliothèque Nationale, Paris)*

up that part of the title dealing with Father Girard and his penitent, but rather adds a sententious explanation at the bottom of
the engraving: 'Man embraces Sensuality because of his tastes,
but loves wisdom out of reason.') It is therefore obvious that the
title page is more complete than the frontispiece, which lacks the
place of publication, the name of the printer and, except for *Le
Décret des sens* and *Ma conversion*, the date of publication. All
this shows that the frontispiece is not limited to the function of
a summary or a prologue, according to position, but that it plays
a key role in the rapid evaluation of the book, which has been
posited as a basic condition throughout this essay, where the
reader flicks through the work, reads the title page and looks at
the frontispiece if there is one. It is on this basis that the choice
is made, and the customer will decide to read (or not) or at least
purchase the work in question. The text could even be said to be
superfluous at this point, existing only as a lure to which is added
the picture and the title page. The crucial part is clearly the
suggestive power of the image.

The picture presented by the frontispiece of the erotic text uses
pounced drawings, stereotypical sketches and patterns that are
then modified and perverted. Cupid, for example, is no longer the
winged cherub with his innocent, smiling face, but rather an
active and impudent little ape, as can be seen from the frontispieces to *Vénus dans le cloître* or *Ma conversion*. As with the
erotic text itself, the image in the frontispiece can proceed by a
profusion of naked bodies, as in the case of *Ma conversion*,
where four naked women offer themselves to a man seated at a
writing desk. And just to show the figure of the writer that these
are no mere sexless divinities, a cherub points with his finger to
the sexual organs of one of the women, while a naked Mercury
enters by what appears to be a window, brandishing a staff. The
engraved bodies do not have the strange, polished perfection of
the gods, but rather the rounded breasts, broad hips and obvious
genitalia that emphasize their physicality and their very real desires.
The image presented on the frontispiece can be rather more limited in its effects, as is the case with *Vénus dans le cloître*, which
shows a half-dressed woman, lifting up her skirts so that a cherub

can fondle her. The position of the woman kneeling on the stool and the voyeuristic aspects of the image are suggestive of the postures described in the erotic text. The reader looking at the frontispiece sees nothing, or rather he sees the cupid who sees. The reader is therefore caught up in a complex delegation of the gaze, translating the reader's position in the reading of the erotic text. The sense is rather less clear than in the frontispiece to *Le Décret des sens*. A single naked female body holds a goose's feather out to a woman in dress typical of the Ancien Régime, her breasts exposed, who is clearly intended to write the title on the book which is held out to her by a sort of winged Mercury whose lyre (is he therefore Apollo?) lies abandoned on the ground. At the woman's feet, the cupid seems to be pulling the flights off the arrows in his quiver. It is remarkable that such a frontispiece should mix realism, mythology and the erotic in a composition that otherwise has little significance. Is it then the case that the Revolution which liberated the texts and which accentuated the crudeness of the titles should exercise such a restraining influence on the pictures that they become rather bland?

These frontispieces also present complementary elements. In *Vénus dans la cloître*, the ground is covered with instruments of mystical penitence, or perhaps less spiritual disciplines, the engraving suggests. From the scroll in the top of the engraving hang a chaplet, whose cross touches the arm of the woman who is exposing herself, and two straps, used for flagellation. At the centre of the same scroll, the laughing head of some satyr or faun underlines the erotic dimension. In *Ma conversion*, above the scroll which contains the title is the head of the fool, with his bell-cap, indicating the excessive nature of the text, as does the place of publication given: Bicêtre, site of a large asylum at the period, and a place of similar symbolic importance to that of the infamous Bedlam. The mediocre quality of the engraving makes it difficult to see what the objects depicted in the frames around the frontispieces are. There are theatrical masks in the frame around the frontispiece of *Ma conversion*, and if you look closely at the frontispiece of *Les Mémoires de Suzon,* what appears to be a trophy made up of two crossed canons is in fact two penises over a woman's sexual organs, with the two sets of ribbons evoking the shape of two pairs of testicles. There is an extensive play of contrasts: the woman at the centre of the engraving seemingly evokes innocence, but her ambiguous gesture, which instead of hiding her nudity, points to the body, an act of designation taken up again by the phallus held by the little angel, which picks up in turn the movement of the scroll and more subtly yet more brutally in the way that the engraving is torn by the ornamental motif.

All in all, this survey shows that it is easy to underestimate the subtle relations between title page and frontispiece, elements which are vital in the organization of the reader's first encounter with the erotic book.

6

Means to an End: the Strategies of Erotic Narrative

It bears repeating once more that the erotic novel (or 'porno-graphic' novel in the sense that we have used the term, a sense hopefully free of moral or qualitative judgements) is aimed at producing a quite particular effect, which is to give rise to the desire for physical pleasure in the reader, to place him or her in a position of tension and lack, the only escape from which can be provided by a recourse to the extra-literary. We have seen that erotic texts give rise to bad habits, being, as Jean-Jacques Rousseau said, the books that one reads only with one hand, or indeed, as Mirabeau put it in rather more lively terms: 'So! Curious and indiscreet friend! You wish to enter into the mysteries of Paphos? Well, then, read, devour and wank!' Either that or it incites the reader into the fevered search for a partner, as the hero of the *Anti-Justine* recounts, inflamed by his reading of the works of the marquis, and who recognized the excitatory effects of that work, only to denounce the cruelty it inspires:

Fontenelle was saying that: 'There is no sorrow that can resist against an hour's reading.' Now, of all the possible reading mat-ter, the most attractive of all is that of erotic works, especially when they are accompanied by expressive pictures. Long since sated with women, *La Justine* by Dsds came into my hands. I was set on fire by the work. I desired pleasure, and it was almost with fury that I bit the breasts of my mount, twisting and pinching her flesh and her arms ... Ashamed of these excesses that resulted from my reading, I created myself an *Erotikon* that would be gentle and savoury, but not cruel, and which excited me to the point that I had commerce a humpbacked, bandy-legged dwarf two feet tall. Take, read and you will do the same.[1]

Rétif's text contradicts some of the details of our analysis of the interferences that can sustain the reading of the erotic text, since he gives a more simplistic account for the effect of reading: the reader does not wish to make use of the same means as the hero of the work; rather, he wishes to experience pleasure too, and the identification stops there. However, Rétif also recognizes the fundamental fact that the reading of the erotic novel leads the reader on. The main thing then is to understand how it can come to produce this remarkable effect, which imposes an illusion that has all the power of reality.

To this end, one could analyse all the erotic novels that contain scenes of reading, and which describe its effects, for it is rare that the erotic novel does not depict its own power at some point in an episode developed to a greater or lesser degree. The mirror effect, the abstract and carefully contrived reflection on the power of such literature, serves to legitimize a writing practice, but also provides some verification of the initiatory role that the book plays as surely as if it were an embrace the reader saw. It is quite right that this period was seen as the triumph of the book. A close reading of episodes taken from *Thérèse philosophe* or *Monsieur Nicolas* is no more illuminating than the exhortations contained in those pastoral letters that railed against the harmful effects of such literature, without explaining how or why. The mystery is the same as surrounds the strange alienation of Don Quixote or Javotte in *Le Roman bourgeois*. If the theme of alienation is recurrent, it is not very explicit and, presented as a simple statement of fact, does not seek to provoke any sort of more profound examination of such a mysterious process. It would be tempting to interpret the position of the reading subject in pathological terms: Don Quixote is mad as far as the priest who burns his library, the crack-brained Jacotte, is concerned. It is not the reader that is on trial here but the book. It is at most the abuse of reading that is responsible for the dangerous or ridiculous.

We cannot apply the same argument to the pornographic novel, for nobody can escape its seductive power. The orders outlined by Tissot and Bienville in their treatises, along with the clerical interdictions, are entirely unequivocal: it is totally forbidden to read them, for nobody can escape from their power. This is entirely different from the *romans de chevalerie, the nouvelles galantes* or even philosophical writings. For the people around him, the *romans de chevalerie* that Don Quixote reads are entirely outmoded and no longer of any interest to anyone; Don Quixote is the only one on whom they have any effect:

> In fine, he gave himself up so wholly to the reading of romances that a-Nights he would pore on it til t'was day, and a-Days he would read on til t'was night; and thus by sleeping little and reading much, the Moisture of his Brain was exhausted to that Degree, that at last he lost the Use of his Reason. A world of disorderly Notions, pick'd out of his books, crouded into his Imagination; and now his Head was full of nothing but Inchantments, Quarrels, Battles, Challenges, wounds, Complaints, Amours, Torments, and abundance of Stuff and Impossibilities; insomuch; that all the Fables and fantastical Tales that he had read seemed to him now as true as the most authentik Histories.[2]

There is a fundamental difference between this and the erotic novel which leaves absolutely no freedom of choice: he who reads the latter succumbs to the power of its illusion. Massillon, in his *Discours inédit sur le danger des mauvaises lectures*, defined this power of conviction carried by erotic literature as exemplifying of the danger of wicked books:

> And you, my brother, claim to read books where the joys of the senses are represented as the highest joy, and these gross passions that bring man back down to the level of the beast as if they were natural needs that one must legitimately satisfy without your

imagination catching fire . . . You claim to read scandalous stories
in which all the ruses of the libertine are laid bare, all the tricks
of debauchery and all the means to commit crime, where the love
of that passion which is the torment of those it enslaves is painted
in such colours that it might even seduce the mature years of
reason, or even old age, where foul creatures devoured by shame-
less fires seek other people to burn with them, representing the
object of their insensate worship as endowed with all the best
qualities imaginable.[3]

It is therefore widely acknowledged that the power of erotic
literature is not shared by any other book, even if it was also
judged to hold a danger by either the religious or the civil authorities. Men and women are both at risk, even if it is thought
that women are more susceptible by nature, as the detractors of
the novel, or Bienville in *De la Fureur utérine*, never neglect to
point out whenever possible. Does this power derive from the
nature of the subject? It would in that case be necessary to recognize that any evocation of amorous pleasures, no matter how
incompetently done, would be enough to have the reader to
experience a violent desire to imitate them. Such a hypothesis is
contradicted by the interference to which the erotic tale is sometimes subject, where the tale would cause no desire in the reader.
It must therefore be admitted that not all erotic tales succeed, and
that there are good ones and bad ones. What determines this
success or failure is the use of the correct narrative strategies, and
so it is with these that we must begin here.

Let us note first of all that the eighteenth-century novel is the
subject of a debate. Questions are asked as to its moral value:
does it distract the reader from more important tasks? Does it
not incite the reader to lose him- or herself in daydreams and
absent-mindedness? Does it not lead the reader to commit sins of
omission? And last of all does it not propose models of behaviour
that are in total contradiction with demands of real life and the
social and moral obligations of the individual? We have seen that
some of the elements of the debate concerning the erotic novel,
the condemnation and rejection of which are dictated by a certain view of the novelistic imaginary and of the relations that

exist between the imagination on the one hand and narrative space on the other. The attempt to deny that the novel can tell or render the truth knows no end. As a work of pure imagination it finds itself incapable of rendering the truth. Subject to narrative conventions and to moral and psychological *a priori*, it would of necessity be distanced from the reality of the world. Forced to have recourse to conventional settings, whether at a level of plot, subject or character, it would be as far removed from reality as history is close to it, for it is in the name of the truth produced by historical discourse that the novel is put on trial. The novelistic illusion creates representations and situations that do not reflect real events and situations, but rather are the product of conventions that the reader recognizes as true by means of cultural conditioning. Diderot's *Jacques le Fataliste* mocks novelistic convention and the codes of verisimilitude that are used in the fiction of the time. He defends himself from the charge that he wished to create a novel. In the course of a rather cursory description of the operation on Jacques' knee, the narrator comments, 'I will spare you all the things that you might find in novels, the comedies of antiquity and in society.'[4] As he repeats so often, the reader finds himself in the very heart of Jacques' loves and not in a novel in the manner of those of the abbé Prévost. As much as to say that the novel of the eighteenth century is troubled in its conscience by its own nature as fiction, as lie and as invention. The only way to reply to its detractors is to hide what it is, and to represent itself as the unadulterated description of real events. Even as he denounces the inventions of the abbé Prévost, Diderot substitutes his own under the pretext that he is doing nothing more than transcribing conversations that genuinely took place between Jacques and his master. Each author in his own way attempts to mask as best he can the fiction that he offers to his public. The first pages of *La Nouvelle Héloïse* are a more successful example of this than most. If we were to believe the authors of all these works, then there would have been an extraordinary number of manuscripts found in trunks (proving that they were not intended for publication) containing authentic memoirs written on their death bed by prominent figures whose exploits would have been of interest to the general public, or indeed of collections of letters, bundles of which are found by pure chance, dusted off and put into some sort of order by an editor who could not resist the pleasure of offering them to a wider readership. Many of the most famous novels of this period belong to this category, claiming that this novel is not in fact a novel at all: *La Vie de Marianne, Le Paysan parvenu, La Religieuse, La Nouvelle Héloïse* or *Les Liaisons dangereuses*, to cite only a few examples, to which one could also add the majority of the erotic novels written in the eighteenth century, all of which are happy to use and abuse the mechanisms by which novels of the period sought to establish some credibility.

The Erotic 'I'

Let us mention a few examples. There are very few epistolary novels apart from *Les Lettres galantes et philosophiques de deux nonnes publiées par un apôtre du libertinage* (1777) or *La Correspondance d'Eulalie ou Tableau du libertinage de Paris ou La Correspondance de Madame Gourdan, dite la Comtesse* (1783). There are, however, an exceptional number of first-person novels, whether their titles are constructed along the model of 'Histoire de . . .' (*Histoire de Dom Bougre* and the many novels derived from that theme) or 'Confessions de . . .' (*Anandria ou Confessions de mademoiselle Sapho*, 1789), or without anything that might lead the future reader to believe that they are written in those forms. Thus, titles such as *L'Anti-Justine, Thérèse philosophe, La Belle Allemande, Le Canapé couleur de feu, Félicia ou Mes fredaines, Hic-et-Hec ou L'Elève des R. P. jésuites d'Avignon, Ma conversion* and *Margot la ravaudeuse* are all first-person novels. The choice of such a form cannot be simply the product of chance or the predominance of a mode of writing, but rather a necessary attempt to fit form and project together.

There is even sometimes a certain excess in the first-person narrative. First-person narratives are frequently grafted onto the main narrative, often narrated by the hero, in the form of insets, which again obey the same enunciatory conditions. *L'Histoire de Dom Bougre*, for example, also contains the 'Récit de Suzon', 'L'Histoire de la Soeur Monique' and then 'La Suite de l'Histoire de la Soeur Monique'. The passage from one tale to another is achieved by means of a meeting and a question. Suzon tells her tale, which is solicited by Saturnin, dealing with her experiences at the convent where she was brought up:

> 'I can see that you have been in a convent. It is such a fine way to shape and form a young lady!'
>
> 'Oh, truly', she replied. 'If I had not been there, I would not know many of the things I know now.'
>
> 'Ah! Tell me then what you know', I continued enthusiastically, 'for I am dying to learn!'[5]

And all that Suzon has to do next is to substitute herself for Saturnin in the role of narrator. The narrative is then distributed between Suzon as the narrator and Sister Monique as her interlocutor, but Saturnin is the true narrator of what is recounted here. Saturnin's function as narrator is quickly dispensed with, as are the verbal and onomastic signals that would permit us to situate the participants in the exchange, in order to give the impression of a conversation or tale taken from real life ('Sister Monique said', or 'I replied', and so on). While those means serve to accentuate the impression of realism, they also theatricize. The situation in these dialogue passages is very close to those in the theatre where the characters speak as if they were alone, even though their words are addressed to an invisible and attentive spectator. When the conversation gives way to a tale, Suzon quite naturally becomes the apparent narrator. Such a dialogue or tale, which in the logic of the narrative belongs to the past (the tale in which they are contained is retrospective), tends to become the narrative present. Everything is read in terms of the contemporary and the immediate present.

Neither the differentiation of temporal structures and narrative voices nor the characterization of each of the interlocutors are actually necessary to the erotic narrative. On the contrary, what is essential is the presence of that voice, of a subject who speaks, as if external to the narrative, as is made possible by the elapsed time and the distance created by memory. The implementation of the mechanism that gives such an effect of presence in the narrative, and thus an impression of realism, is particularly apparent in the foreword of *L'Histoire de la soeur Monique*. It is Sister Monique who speaks through Suzon's mouth, as Saturnin the narrator affirms. 'However passionate this sister might appear to you, I fear that my words can give only an inadequate impression. What little time I spent with her gave me an impression that it is impossible to render faithfully.'[6] The inset narrative confesses its duplicity, being both the same and different. It has no explanatory function in the logic of the narrative as a whole, serving above all to legitimize the displacement in space and the repetition of the erotic narrative. It offers the promise of renewal, a promise that it cannot deliver, since, despite all the appearances of diversity, it is nonetheless a depiction of the same. It is for that reason without doubt that the narrative exhausts itself in trying to appear different from itself without ever succeeding. Without any differentiation it confesses its incapacity to create a genuine diversity of bodies and embraces. However, from this weakness comes strength, since it is there that the necessary condition for the ultimate pleasure of the reader is created.

We could make a list of the interpolations and framing devices in most of the great texts of erotic literature. Very few deviate from the general rule of reiteration under the disguise of apparent heterogeneity conferred by the encasing of stories told by the various characters. We might well cite the story recounted by Madame Bois-Laurier in *Thérèse philosophe* and the innumerable stories, accounts and histories, all of varying length and function, which punctuate Rétif de la Bretonne's *Anti-Justine*. One might even wonder whether the novel's incompleteness (it ends on a mysterious and incomplete 'Elle . . .') might not constitute, despite itself, the sign of an ever-present possibility of beginning the tale again with a new inset narrative, the arrival on the stage of new partners, a redistribution of couples and figures. It is in the very nature of the erotic novel never to finish, in the very image of that desire that it seeks to arouse and which is reborn in the precise moment of its satisfaction.

As we shall see, the inset narratives participate in this mirror construction, which is so vital to the writing of pornography, where it is a question of indicating quite clearly that the object shown is seen by a gaze that is designated as looking. They also give the illusion of progression in the narrative on a dramatic level, a real sequence of sudden changes which create a narrative tension, and last of all a multiplicity of highly individuated characters. This illusion is vital to the hall of mirrors behind which hides the nudity and barrenness of the erotic novel. For it is that narrative voice, almost too familiar to the reader, which is then falsely diversified by the reprises provided by the inset narratives in order to attest to the multiple presence of desire. However, even though there is a real effect on the reader, just as in the traditional novel of the period, such a process also reveals that the characters are entirely devoid of any personality. They are nothing more than pure functions. Whether a given woman is young or old, blonde or brunette, short or tall, beautiful or ugly, thin or plump is of little importance, since it is the desire of the reader alone that gives him access to the novelistic universe. That the heroes of the pornographic novels belong to this world, which is paradoxically entirely that of the flesh and yet also highly abstract, is entirely a function of their capacity to experience pleasure. For their destiny in the novel is reduced totally to that moment of *jouissance*, which is expected, desired and finally conquered. Apart from that they are nothing. We learn much more about their anatomical peculiarities than about their character. Here there is no trace of psychological depth. The hero of the pornographic novel, the reader's intimate companion, has no memory. His moment of *jouissance*, as thunderous as it might be, leaves no trace whatsoever – it is forgotten as soon as its is felt so that desire can be born again, tenacious and triumphant. There is neither memory nor love. The hero is a perpetual absence and a perpetual beginning again. If one voice makes itself heard beneath the various other illusory tones, then that is a product of the fact that the hero under the diversity of appearances, even sexual difference, is nothing more than a manifestation of desire and the feverish quest for pleasure. In the act of reading they are all subsumed by that one voice that tirelessly speaks of possession and pleasure.

That which might appear as a fault in fact turns out to be a functional necessity: the absence of psychological analysis, and even of any character psychology, the unity of the narrative voice, despite the various first-person inset narratives, are some of the elements that allow the reading of pornography to have its effect. There are no states of mind therefore, but rather states of the body; no reflection on oneself, but rather a single action that is always the same, the action of desiring bodies. There is one first-person discourse which does not attempt to diversify the narrative voices, but which looks to establish a privileged relationship with the reader, a certain intimacy proper to the intrusive and voyeuristic reading act of the erotic novel. Similarly, we must also attempt to understand the episodic construction of the erotic novel: there is nothing that links the episodes together except the desire and the pleasure which recur in the form of a *leitmotif*. The mechanism is quite simple: it is either the partner, the place or the positions that change. One episode can offer several figures of love by augmenting the number of partners given up to their frenzied activities. From a structural point of view, there is no change from one episode to the next: the tempo, the progression and the dénouement are always the same. Moreover, it is inadvisable that they should change. The reader would not, generally speaking, wish for such a thing, and the erotic effect of the text would be severely compromised by it. For one of the paradoxes of the pornographic novel is that the reader knows what to expect, and it is indeed far from clear that the reader would wish for anything new or unexpected. The combinations, and even the deviations, only have any meaning insofar as they lead to still greater pleasures. The hero of the erotic novel who was disappointed in his expectation would become a figure more from either vaudeville or some story of a return to the path of virtue than from his own genre. Even if he is subject to such treatment that it exhausts him to the point of renouncing sexual pleasure (and such is the end of Dom Bougre himself), then this is nothing more than the proof of the absolute availability and readiness of its sexual partners, a fact of which the pornographic imaginary seeks confirmation in his own reading. The episodes can be seen as separate to the point that they could be excised to furnish material for so many autonomous tales throughout the nineteenth century.

THE READER AS INTRUDER

The episodes of the erotic novel impose themselves on the reader as so many fixed images, or more exactly as a *tableau vivant* which he is the only one to see. Every description attracts his moonstruck gaze. There is nothing less suited to the practice of reading out loud than the erotic novel, a genre that demands solitude and silence. It is there alone that one is plunged into the book as if in a darkened room.

There is a paradox, of course. If the narrative is in the first person, then its function is to make the reader see, and to mark out that which is to be seen. Everything happens as if the narrative voice played the role of the guide and was used to point to particular elements in the picture. Hence a writing that captivates the attention by a concentration on the essential details, by means of a succession of set pieces, by the dizzying and obsessive magnification of details. Of all the bodies engaged in the amorous encounter, the reader perceives only the desiring sex. If there is any exchange of words, then that is to compliment someone on their beauty, or some other physical feature, or to seek to engage somebody in further effort, or to call on someone to give them pleasure. The erotic narrative operates by dissociation and parcelling and proceeds thenceforth by means of hyperbole. Thus the woman, described first of all as a whole (and whether she is beautiful or not is entirely secondary, as we have seen), finishes by being reduced to a single part of her body, which can nonetheless be multiplied by all the means available.

The narrator has a double role, both describing and acting. Or, more exactly, he describes what he sees and describes himself acting. In the manner of the engraving, he throws light on that which should be momentarily glimpsed. Everything else is in shadow. There is therefore a voice which serves the gaze, and which makes explicit the elements of the tableau that is presented or which is in the process of being constructed. As much as to say that he plays the role of intermediary, of another reader. The novel organizes its reading in the form of manifold delegation of the gaze. It is not unusual for the hero to surprise a couple (such episodes can be found in *Thérèse philosophe, Dom Bougre, Hic-et-Hec* and *Le Rideau levé ou L'Education de Laure*, and recurs at several points in the novels of Rétif de la Bretonne). He spies through a gap or a hole made in a partition. His gaze perceives only the amorous scene or the fragment of their bodies focalized to the extreme. Here is an example seen through the eyes of Mirabeau's heroine, Laure:

> Half an hour had scarcely gone by before Lucette fell sound asleep, and he took me in his arms and carried me to his bed. I was surprised by this change in arrangements and my curiosity was instantly aroused. I sat up for a moment after and ran lightly to the door, and moved the curtain that covered its panes. I was quite astounded to see Lucette entirely naked from the waist up. What beautiful breasts! Two half-globes snowy-white, in the middle of each two little buds of a deeper tint, rested against her chest; firm as ivory, they only moved with her breathing. My father looked at them, fondling them, kissing them, sucking at them: nothing awoke her. Soon he had taken off all her clothes, and moved her to the edge of the bed facing the door through which I was looking. He lifted up her nightgown. I saw two thighs of alabaster, round and soft, which he drew apart.[7]

This passage from *Le Rideau levé ou L'Education de Laure* illustrates the role of the furtive observer that devolves to the narrating hero in the early part of the novel. It also illustrates the fragmenting of the body subject to the gaze, as well as the fragmentation of the action itself and the absence of significance given to the various acts, which gives a convincing impression of the

ingenuousness of the young girl watching. This is the only fundamental difference between the gaze of the reader falling on the
thing described and its *mise en texte* by the intermediary of the
hero himself. These episodes of furtive voyeurism which generally
open the tale constitute a sort of indication of position, an in-
junction addressed to the reader. In the episodes that follow, the
strategy attached to the gaze changes. We move from an intrusive
and illicit voyeurism (rather akin to the position of the reader,
shut out from the wild pleasures of the bodies on the page) to the
deliberate eye that appraises those bodies that offer themselves
up. There is no need to hide any more; rather, the gaze makes its
presence felt: it is described in order to be perceived, noticed and
interpreted as a solicitation and an offer. The description of the
other's body takes on the coldness of the connoisseur or even a
clinical precision of the livestock trade. There then intervenes a
vocabulary that can be either technical or crude. We can see this
in operation in a passage from *La Philosophie dans le boudoir*,
where Dolmancé gives Eugénie some instruction in practical
biology.

By imposing a certain exteriority on the text as part of the
reading process, the narrative device does allow for a certain
degree of play. The reader confronted with the rather neutral
impression garnered by an innocent eye is required to decode a
fractured and fragmented series of gestures and to give it back its
full meaning. Looking over the shoulder of the child narrator at
this spectacle intended for adult eyes, he invests the raw account
with his experience and his knowledge in matters of love. This
sense of superiority at the expense of the other characters is not
devoid of pleasure. Such an analysis is valid not merely for the
opening of *Le Rideau élevé ou L'Education de Laure*, but also
for all the opening episodes of the erotic novel of education.
Diderot used the procedure in *La Religieuse* when the novice,
Suzanne Simonin, describes, without understanding their significance, the shudders of the Mother Superior, from which the reader
is to understand that she is on the verge of climax. From this
interpretation of the text, which implies a considerable participation on the part of the reader, one moves to the sequence of

episodes itself, to a position which is entirely its reverse. The text requires no commentary at all; it is explicit, and there is no need to translate or to transpose. The reader is no longer in the position of the voyeur, attentive but ignorant, but rather he has become an actor in the embrace itself. The only voyeur that remains is the reader confronted with the raw description of physicality.

We have already spoken of the ambiguous and paradoxical position of the narrator, an actor who must at the same time describe both himself and the other. In the logic of a first-person narrative, the descriptions of sexual activity should be formulated from the narrative point of view of the hero, but then is not the moment of orgasm, of *jouissance*, an abolition of exteriority, a loss of consciousness and the ability to maintain the sort of distances implied by the position of the narrator as we have stated it? How can one produce the effect of that moment, and yet also present from the outside the moment when being collapses into the sensation to such a point that a position of exteriority to the narrative could no longer be maintained? There is an obvious contradiction. The first-person narrative is necessary in order to establish a sort of intimacy with the reader and to construct the narrative as the individualized utterance, in the image of a highly personalized relationship with the other's moment of pleasure, perceived as a sort of guilty intrusion. Yet at the same time it represents by its very form, which is necessarily distanced, the negation of the exact thing of which it claims to give an account. The temporal distance and the reported narrative cannot legitimize by themselves that narration of a cold and studied climax. Such a narration oscillates between the dry observation of facts, translated by the use of the verb *jouir* ('to come') in a rather literal sense, the uncontrolled language of that moment or yet again the external description of the revels in which the narrator is both actor and witness.

The subtlety of the narrative would then consist not merely in not choosing and making use of this triple register. The repeated use of the verb *jouir* and its various synonyms is one of the most simple and immediate ways of describing the moment. The narrative moves from the generic usage to commentary and gloss by means of gestures, language and physiological changes that the narrator perceives in the partner. In addition, there is the spontaneous and even inarticulate speech of that moment, where language breaks down into cries, sighs and half-intelligible words. The description can be that of the narrator or the partner, the two sometimes mixing even as their bodies are joined, as is the case in this passage from *Ma conversion*:

> Fuck! The fury seizes me, and I become heated. My heel against a column, I press her and lift her up. There she goes . . . Ah! My friend! My Little one! My dear heart! . . . I'm dying . . . Ah! I didn't think that it could happen any more . . . Such a long time . . . Ah! Ah! Ah! I'm coming . . . oh God, I'm coming . . . May the devil take me if her convulsions did not hold me in the sweet bliss of illusion a full five minutes. The old devil came as if she were a woman of thirty, and it took her a long time to recover from it, being exhausted, emptied. As for me, I was in a fine sweat . . . [8]

We could add to the list of passages that one could cite in support of this argument. Note that it is the inarticulable experience of the climax of the other that dominates, for it is by this means that is best expressed the double position of the hero who is at the same time both actor – and what an actor – and witness.

It is not unusual that the narrative should present the narrator as the voyeur himself, which is not entirely implausible. Not that this is a criticism in the name of some notion of reality, but rather a reminder of the imperative demands of narrative coherence. Thus, to better produce the effect, even while denying it (for can one experience and be witness to one's own orgasm?), the narrator puts himself in such a position, or conserves a sufficient degree of lucidity to observe quite minutely the climax of his partner. The body then appears as an instrument for pleasure from which the head is entirely independent. What is even more extraordinary still, but which is forced upon the narrative by its own logic, is that the narrator becomes the voyeur in couples where he takes an active part. It is not unusual for the narrative to use the device of a menage à trois in order to justify the double

position of actor and witness. In the tangle of bodies minutely
described by the text, the narrator assigns himself an intermediary position where he can act, see and be seen. The linking of
bodies is not simply part of the construction of a space for fantasy, it is the possibility of a discourse essential to the reading of
the erotic text.

The Erotic Tableau

We must finally attempt to give some account of the notion of
the tableau, which I have already used several times in the course
of this essay, and which is vital to the production of desire in the
erotic text. This is a key notion, but also a contradictory one in
some ways, as is shown by the ambiguity inherent in the positions dictated by the narrative. There is a tableau for the simple
reason that there is a setting, the inscription of the bodies into the
space they saturate. The tableau exists only by dint of this capacity to occupy space in the narrative and by means of the various
forms of emphasis that give certain parts greater space still, such
as enlargement; the prominence given a sexual organ by means
of a few lines here and there, a sigh or a moment of fainting are
almost the only things permitted to exist in the narrative. The
placing in the tableau of the amorous coupling belongs to the
realm of the fixed image, almost of hallucination, one might even
say, and also to that of the ritual of love. In order to arrive at
that end, it uses descriptions by means of those delegations of the
gaze that we have already discussed, and those devices of language that make present the fevered pursuit of pleasure. For it is
the spoken word that serves to give some dynamic to this space.
In *Jacques le Fataliste*, Diderot creates a descriptive space without there being any description of the operation itself: advice is
given to those assisting, places are assigned and instruments asked
for. Speech accompanies sexual activity in the same fashion:
exclamations wise or foolish, demands made out of desire or in
the unstoppable rise of physical pleasure. 'Ah! gently, my dear
Toinette, not so fast! Ah! You mischief! I'm dying. Faster, faster.

God! I'm dying!' cries out the monk Ambroise in *Dom Bougre* when he is taken by surprise by the young Saturnin. Similar passages can be found in the majority of erotic novels. There are a good number in *Thérèse philosophe* or in *Le Rideau levé*. The system is always the same: a certain moment is evoked rather than described. This very absence of any description conveys the loss of consciousness, the effect of orgasm itself. And it is no accident if the word *mourir* is constantly used in these passages, for it represents, with the suspension marks, the incomplete propositions, the only means to render present, from both a visual and a semantic point of view, the hero's total abandon.

Such passages also provide the means to reintroduce an interpretative participation of the reader, a participation that is substantial in the initial episodes, and which, once the hero has acquired a certain experience in love, seems to have become useless. The words pronounced constitute a discourse which is not directly descriptive, but permits the substitution of the reader for the narrator charged to witness and to describe. The essential element in the presentation of the amorous embrace is perhaps this two-way process, this substitution of reader for narrator and narrator for reader in a complex but efficiently managed exercise in direction.

The effect of distance, rather than distancing (the distinction is of some importance), is essential in the representation of sexual activity. It permits the reader to construct an image in which he does not participate, but which nonetheless is as powerful as an obsession. This visual power of the erotic tableau is essentially a product of the distance produced by the narrative strategies of the erotic tale. The words of the various partners create a closed narrative space, devoid of any broader horizon and limited to the characters themselves. It also allows for the momentary elimination of the narrator (even if he is taking part in the activity depicted), in order to accentuate the effect of closure and the complete devotion to the act. The key thing is to show by speaking that there can be no other discourse than the desire for pleasure and the plenitude of *jouissance* itself. The disappearance of the descriptive speech of the narrator is therefore no unhappy accident: it corresponds to the necessity of the process of eroticization. Any words other than the one that serves or expresses the moment of *jouissance* becomes superfluous. There is nothing but cries, commands and furore.

This status of the spoken word in the erotic novel is sufficiently remarkable to warrant some further investigation. The speech offered by the characters, whether it is the narrator or one of his interlocutors, is always strictly functional, or at least should be if the erotic novel is to remain faithful to its premises. This functionality is nonetheless also diverse and changing, creating intimacy at first and finishing with the confusion of the various layers of different voices with the voice of the principal narrator. As a result, the reader has the impression that the narrative exists only for him, and to such a point that it is not unusual (as is the case in *Ma conversion*) for the novel to speak to the reader by name and be constructed, like *Jacques le Fataliste* (but without the same perverse dysfunctionality), in the form of a dialogue between a narrator and an impatient listener, who asks questions and is often called to witness. 'Up until now, my friend, I have been a good-for-nothing. I have run after beauties and I have played hard to get. At this moment, virtue returns to my heart. I will only fuck for money henceforth, and I will advertise myself as the sworn stallion to all women on my return and I will teach them the joys of the arse for a certain amount per month.'[9] Such is the opening of *Ma conversion*, with a dialogue apparently taken from life by the reader himself, and who, in the huge silences left by the interlocutor, will come to assume an important role. The words of the narrator are addressed to a fictive interlocutor, and one who says very little all in all, since, although his interventions are quite frequent at the beginning of the narrative, they nonetheless disappear entirely by the end. By this means the tale inscribes itself into a tradition of male confidences, that is to say a wider cultural practice again also amply attested in *Jacques le Fataliste*.

Creating intimacy and confidence, the narrator's speech, which is the final receptacle for all other voices in the narrative, also serves by means of a dialectic of effacement and absence of other voices to create the closed and blind space for the fantastic representation of those bodies offered up and represented. Intimacy and closure in the same breath, therefore. The thing is to reduce the narrative space to these provocative, desiring and active bodies. The word finally comes to theatricize and to set the scene, even when it is confused, incoherent or imperious in its demands. The disappearance of the narrator places the reader in the position of a direct but distant witness, to the point that the narrative becomes theatrical. There is no more narration, simply replies with stage instructions, as in Sade's *La Philosophie dans le boudoir*, or *Vénus dans le cloître ou La Religieuse en chemise* or a narrative in the form of conversations, which places the reader in an external position but which often then leads the erotic novel to give way to philosophical didacticism – a flaw in quite a few pages of *Thérèse philosophe*, for example.

The sexual gymnastics of the group has a capital importance in the erotic novel. It organizes the various figures into a complex architecture which mixes and joins bodies, and which finally confuses them. The creation of the tableau here becomes rather paradoxical: each body unites with the neighbouring body and thus there is a sort of closed figure, never described as a whole, and always perceived from the centre constituted by the body of the narrator himself, and then across the other bodies, which are individualized, fragmented and dissociated. The narrator's body becomes the final conduit for all *jouissance*, and draws its ultimate pleasure from the pleasure of others. The group is then conceived of as a single body engaged in the work of desire and pleasure, or as a machine for transferring movement. For the description seeks to reconcile the pose (a term used consistently in Sade's works) representing the immobility and the hallucinatory fixity of the tableau vivant, as well as the vibrant, breathless movement of the pleasure that is sought and attained. This paradoxical duality of the use of the tableau in the erotic novel can be related to the use of the tableau in the bourgeois drama, as defined by Diderot in his *Entretien sur le fils naturel*. It is presented as a suspension in the time-scheme, a point of contact between the theatrical and pictorial representation, a representation of movement and of the capturing of the truth in a single moment. The stage instruction provided by Beaumarchais in Act II scene iv, of *Le Mariage de Figaro* is a good example of this:

> [The countess is] seated, she holds the paper to follow the words. Suzanne, behind her armchair, begins the introduction while reading the notes over her mistress' shoulder. The page stands in front of her, his eyes lowered. The scene duplicates that of the beautiful print made from Vanloo's painting, entitled *Conversation in Spain*.[10]

There could be no better demonstration of the paradox of fixity and movement, of the unfolding and the instant.

In the tableau of the group of bodies the bodies invade and take over all the available space, thought of as a single body and a single moment of *jouissance*. The communion is so perfect that everything becomes one, body and pleasure. By this constant affirmation of how the bodies combine, the bodies become rather abstract, as if making way for the absent reader, who is nonetheless invited to participate in this moment. The reader no longer knows what to look at and the tableau escapes from all logic, roles are modified and permuted, and each individual is simultaneously active and passive. Each part becomes a representative of the whole, and each body is reduced to that part that will produce, provoke or experience *jouissance*. A single gesture then gives the scene its movement in a description that pushes the figure of metonymy to its very limits.

The erotic tableau presents only a very superficial view of pleasure. Bodies penetrate one another without anything being said of their organic interiority, which is one of the limits that the sadian text transgresses by its descriptions of the more visceral aspects of sexual intimacy. Everything is reduced to a sort of action painting, to an unformulated discourse of *jouissance*. The reader-spectator must see and hear. The erotic novel, even as it constructs the narrative space as a single body, as a machine for the production of pleasure, nonetheless remains a depiction of forms and appearances. One might well be tempted to say that it represents a sort of shadow play.

On the Illustration of the Erotic Text

While an exhaustive examination would be impossible, some discussion of the iconography of the erotic novel is required, returning first of all to the title page, which we have already examined. It is not unusual for a novel to be described as illustrated ('avec figures'). Since the title page has given sufficient indication of the character of the work in question, we can measure the sort of role that such an indication must play. Detractors of the erotic novel constantly denounce the effect of such images, while its admirers never stop praising it. For the latter, these images represent an added attraction, which means that the subject of illustration has to be taken into account when examining the desire that the erotic novel seeks to produce. The relationship between the illustration and the erotic text is complex. Either it serves to illustrate a particular episode, or it offers something more generally pornographic that has no particular relation to the text in hand. It is not unusual for different novels to have basically the same illustrations, without any apparent demur on the part of the readers. Such a practice shows the repetitive and codified quality of the erotic novel. The situations and the episodes are determined more by the dictates of genre than by the specific nature of any given work. It also proves that the characters are not at all individualized. They are conceived of as fictions and are therefore interchangeable, with scarcely any features that could personalize them. The rather banal illustration that could serve in a variety of works renders the anonymity of the heroes themselves. As much as to say that this imagery should not be judged by its originality or the quality of its execution, but, rather like the licentious text itself, making due allowance for the differences that there inevitably are between the textual and the pictorial, in term of their function in the work. Thus the lack of originality, far from being a fault, certainly corresponds to a mode proper to erotic iconography.

There is also an illustration that follows the text, as in *Ma conversion, Dom Bougre* or *Thérèse philosophe*, which serves to illustrate particular episodes. In *Ma conversion* the picture is accompanied by a brief fragment of text; sometimes there is more, with a title according to the different types of women the hero encounters. There are therefore engagements with 'the religious devotee', 'the baroness', 'Agnès' and so on. Even if the illustration in *Dom Bougre* is specific in this manner, then there is neither legend nor title. Like *La Nouvelle Héloïse* or Rétif de la Bretonne's *Monsieur Nicolas, Thérèse philosophe* has a table to explain the nature of the 'sixteen prints contained in this work'. The first of these is the frontispiece, while the fifteen others refer to precise episodes which are summarized. 'Second print: Thérèse is playing with boys and girls of her own age in an attic. The effects of a precocious development'; 'third print: the pleasure-seeking Father Dirrag flagellates his penitent'; 'fourth print: he experiences great pleasure as a result: the properties of the cord of St Francis'. This description of the prints shows that the organization in the erotic novel is no different from the more general sorts of illustrated works of fiction. There is the same desire to stay close to the text, and to follow its various twists and turns – yet a further proof that the erotic novel differs little from more traditional novelistic forms.

The analysis of the engraving confirms the hypotheses that have been advanced for the analysis of the narrative strategies of the erotic text. Let us note first of all the absence of any individualization of the characters, no more personalized than those found in the illustrations where it is impossible to recognize the hero, or even to differentiate the different partners. Suzon, Sister Monique, Toinette: they are all so many naked bodies, anonymous and functionalized. The same thing applies to the male figures, apart from a few cases where a particular individual role is attributed to them: the voyeur or the body being looked at. The only exception is perhaps the monk, who is recognizable by his tonsure. Anti-clericalism is present even in the prints.

The images are realistic, insofar as the sexual organs are portrayed. We are a long way from those smooth and polished classical forms. There is nothing but buxom breasts, erect penises, the discreet show of public hair and the ample buttocks of the female characters. Yet the sexual act as such is not directly represented. Often the superimposed bodies mask the events that are taking place, but more commonly the engraving represents the preparation for sexual activity, making the confrontation that precedes it rather more frozen. Taking these constraints as a point of departure, the engravings use as much variety as they can, although it is difficult to count more than four bodies. There is also a certain realism, for, whatever the postures represented and the architecture constructed, we always remain with the instant before the actual coupling. Therein lies without doubt the graphic equivalent of a basic prohibition and of the necessity to depict the bodies involved at a distance. However, the image is only apparently set back in the text. Indeed, it is perfectly suited to the text, each conserving its particularities and its overdetermining representational constraints.

For it is true that the engraving obeys the imperatives of the tableau. Everything calls for and solicits the gaze of the reader, but in an indirect manner. There is a framing of the image that places the spectator outside the engraving, at a certain distance. Not one of the characters represented might be in a position to look outside of the engraving itself. Instead, the gazes of the characters are concentrated on the bodies within the frame of the pictures, as if the engraving wished to underline its closure and its total obliviousness to the person looking at it. As much as to say that by its organization, and by the relations depicted between the characters, the engraving wishes to make apparent the invasive, intrusive act committed by the person looking at it. We therefore have a picture of naked people offered up without one single detail giving away a complicity that is nonetheless acknowledged. The same act of solicitation can be seen as one of the principal strategies of the erotic text itself.

And yet, the more one looks, the more the engravings represent a device to set off the bodies offered up to the hidden observer. Against all logic, therefore, there is depicted a three-quarter profile of bodies in the instant before the act of love itself. The engraved figures display themselves to both their partner and the silent and absent spectator who flicks through the book. These rumps, these breasts and these sexual organs have no erotic function internal to the engraving, but rather are subject to the silent surveillance of the spectator. It is for the benefit of that unexpected gaze that the distribution of light and shade in the engraving is organized. What is striking is the insistent presence of windows through which the light enters the engravings contained in *Ma conversion*. This feature does not correspond to the logic of the narrative, which usually refers to closed spaces, cut off from all communication with the outside world. Such a presence has no *raison d'être* except for the light that it throws on the bodies depicted. The flesh is engorged with light and becomes a point of dazzling whiteness in a grey and black space. If the window dominates, beyond the illustrations in *Ma conversion*, then they can be replaced by a lighting effect that is not actually justified by the picture itself, somewhat as if the illumination had no other source than the gaze of the reader, like a shaft of light that suddenly enters and disturbs a moment of intimacy.

This presence of the gaze, a palpable but almost uncertain reality of the voyeur in the scenic disposition of the erotic illustration, is symbolically indicated by an outsider witnessing the moment. There must be some count given of the busts with their piercing eyes, or the overmantles decorated with interesting scenes, or the troubled but attentive faces of servant-girls, looking through a half-open door. Lovers are never alone in the world; rather, a gaze always presides over their pleasures. It can even happen that, by means of some spectacular contortion, the body of the participant can become the witness of his own embrace. As much as to say that the engraving in some ways follows the text to the letter. In the fourth print from *Thérèse philosophe* there is an unexpected enlargement; an excessive focalization means that the space of the picture is almost entirely occupied by the sexual organs of Father Dirrag. There we have the visual equivalent of the dismemberment and parcelling so well attested in the strategies of the accompanying text.

Although this survey has emphasized the gaps and disjunctions in the relation of the illustration to the text, and especially the imperfect saturation of the visual space by the bodies, it cannot modify the basic unity of the pornographic novel, where text serves image as image serves text.

Conclusions

Throughout this study the goal has been to find out how the erotic (or pornographic, as we term it nowadays) novel achieves its effect. Not that the designation of pornography should be understood, as I have already said, as a condemnation of the bad taste of its readers; nor, on the contrary, should the reading of such works be understood as an act of libertarian defiance. By means of this analysis I have sought to elaborate a model that is applicable to all fictional and novelistic forms, of which the erotic novel is merely a species. The value of the erotic novel is that it appears as the model for a fiction that succeeds in creating an illusion just as powerful as reality itself, as the effects felt prove.

In this description of the project I have undertaken, the reader will have detected a certain nostalgia, not for some mythical Golden Age of pornographic literature which might have existed in the eighteenth century, but rather for an era which perhaps never existed, other than in the desire to write and to tell stories, and where literature, in competition with the real world, could truly deceive the reader. There is therefore some nostalgia for a certain magic in an all-powerful writing where the author would be God, for, well before Mallarmé and the proponents of a writing that could create reality through language, the authors of pornographic novels participated in this belief in the limitless powers of literature and put them into practice. Indeed, they were like those gods said to create by naming. Pornographic literature is therefore perhaps the most audacious, the most presumptuous promise that all literature can offer, and perhaps even that art can offer: to produce something that the reader or viewer takes for reality.

The attentive reader will have spotted another nostalgia in these pages: the nostalgia for a Golden Age of reading. Not for an era when the printed word enjoyed its supreme triumph and constituted perhaps the unique form of cultural communication, nor even for a period when pornographic literature would have been the dominant form. The nostalgia presented is rather that for a passionate and naïve reading. This largely hypothetical reconstruction of the reading of erotic literature seeks to recall a past time: that of adolescence where the books in question were not, fortunately or unfortunately, pornographic, but rather when reading was something immediate and without distance, in total forgetfulness of the outside world. I remember being totally unaware of my grandmother's voice, trying to call me away from the book I was reading. The professional readers that we become, attentive to questions of form, suspicious of artifice, alive to the pleasures of elegant construction, appreciative of writerly craft, can only regret the passing of our fascinated naïveté. And why not imagine a prehistory of reading where all readers would have been like these charmed adolescents, rather like the first film audiences, who rushed screaming towards the exits, overturning tables and chairs, when the train entered the station billowing clouds of steam. The reading of the pornographic novel, such as we have analysed and reconstructed it, constitutes one of the main means of getting an impression of the primitivism of these readers, and by that means to fill in some of the gaps in our cultural history: the emotion felt, however one will, and despite all the efforts of the historians of reading, in that physical and yet also interior world of readers without whom all literary history would be mutilated and abstract.

The two nostalgias that I have evoked are far from independent from one another, but rather are linked. The fascination of the reader points back to a mystery and to the powers of the author. The two cannot be thought of separately. An analysis such as the one that is drawing to a close here would also seek to remind the reader, by means of the very particular case of pornographic literature and the conditions in which the text is approached, that the relation between the reader and the printed word is complex and cannot be reduced to the continuous reading of letters, paragraphs and chapters. The book seduces by means of its cover, its title and its title page before the reader is swallowed up by the text itself. Like many others, I have just as vivid a memory of the covers of *Fantomas*, sold for 65 centimes by Fayard, as I do for the adventures of Fantomas, Juve and Fandor themselves. The reading of a book begins a good way before the first line of the first chapter, as the means by which the pornographic book seeks to sell itself proves.

And to finish with these various nostalgias and all these imperious reminders, one might wonder if the pornographic novel, sketched out in functional form, can really exist. Is it not indeed the case that the work is always the victim of those sorts of interference which I have used to disqualify texts that are often all too quickly placed in the canon of such literature? Thus the pornographic novel would be a sort of impossible project, a horizon never attained, a shimmering virtuality. There are fragments of eroticism that are always shadowed by the danger of distraction, whether from philosophical material or from psychological, sentimental or physiological reasons. As a last survivor of this literary practice, here presented as a form of asceticism or a road to perfection. The difficulty of the pornographic novel in being the printed trace of its idea brings it somewhat closer to a more general practice which is that of literature breaking its own rules and betraying its aims. It is rather, as if in order to return to that vast constellation, that the erotic novel owed it to itself to be nothing more than itself, in its own way absent at the last.

Appendix

On the basis of the bibliographies to which I have already referred – those of Guillaume Apollinaire, Pascal Pia and Sarane
Alexandrian, but also *L'Anthologie historique des lectures érotiques* by Jean-Jacques Pauvert (Paris, 1979) – it would not be un-
thinkable to compile a relatively exhaustive list of pornographic
literature in the eighteenth century, although this is not my intention. Even less would it be my intention to make a list of all the
reprints and new editions. By means of the study of a few titles,
I wish to underline the importance of the genre during the
Enlightenment. The quality of the names cited – leaving aside
Sade – should provide sufficient demonstration of this. It is quite
possible to get an idea of the works that provided models for the
genre, and which it would be tempting to read as a simple list of
novels that were never equalled, although often imitated. For the
most part, these have been re-edited throughout the nineteenth
century, and constitute an essential basis for pornographic literature of the period. It would be wrong to consider the list as fixed
and monolithic. The pornographic novel did not cease to evolve
and to borrow material from the mainstream of novelistic writing, or from a variety of genres, when it is not the only genre in
which the writer published. In this case it represents a sort of
place for exchange, but what it gains in philosophy, in narrative
virtuosity or even in humour, it loses in its effectiveness as a
pornographic novel. The purists might regret such a loss. Here,
therefore, are a few titles that might give some impression of the

scale of the production of pornographic literature in the eighteenth century. As for the quality of the material, I offer no judgement, since literary quality is far from central to the pornographic novel. This list serves only as a guide, and has no value from a bibliographical point of view. It should be used in conjunction with and as a supplement to the titles mentioned in chapter 6.

Translator's note: Where possible I have indicated translations for the works listed. However, the reliability and quality of some of the earlier translations of these French texts is rather variable, since earlier examples were not conceived of as scholarly renderings of the originals, but rather often disseminated in limited runs through private book-clubs. English versions from the nineteenth century have a textual history as complex and elusive as that of their continental models, and a guide to these can be found in Peter Mendes' *Clandestine Erotic Fiction in English 1800–1930: a Bibliographical Study* (Aldershot: Scolar Press, 1993). As often as not, English versions drew on French texts and remodelled them, as is the case with Rétif de la Bretonne's *L'Anti-Justine*, which formed the basis for *The Double Life of Cuthbert Cockerton* (1798).[1] For a survey of the history of the translation and influence of French pornography in England, see Patrick J. Kearney, *A History of Erotic Literature* (London: Macmillan, 1982).

Alexis Piron, *Ode à Priape* (1710).
Louis-Charles Fougeret de Monbron, *Le Canapé couleur de feu* (1741).
Baculard d'Arnaud, *L'Art de foutre ou Paris Foutant* (1741).
Jean-Charles Gervaise de la Touche, *Histoire de Dom B...*, *portier des Chartreux* (1741); (translated as *The History of Father Saturnin alias Dom Bxxx alias Gouberdom, Porter of the Charterhouse of Paris* [for details, see Mendes, p. 153]).
Godard d'Aucour, *Thémidore ou Mon histoire et celle de ma maîtresse* (1745).
Claude-Henri Fusée, abbot of Voisenon, *Le Sultan Misapouf* (1746).
——, *Zulmis et Zelmaïde* (1747).
Jean-Baptiste de Boyer, marquis of Argens, *Thérèse philosophe*

(1748); (translated as *The Philosophical Theresa*, Société des bibliophiles étrangers, 1900 [for details, see Mendes, p. 325]).

Le Chevalier de La Morlièe, *Les Lauriers ecclésiastiques ou Les Campagnes de l'abbé T . . .* (1748).

Crebillon fils, *Les Tableaux des moeurs du temps et dans les différents âges de la vie* (1750).

Fougeret de Monbron, *Margot la ravaudeuse* (1750).

Granval fils, *La Nouvelle Messaline* (1750, theatrical production).

Gabriel Senac de Meilhan, *La Foutromanie* (1775).

Mirabeau, *Ma Conversion ou Le Libertin de qualité* (1783).

——, *Le Rideau levé ou L'Education de Laure* (1785); (translated as *The Curtain Drawn Up or The Education of Laura from the French of Count Mirabeau*, London, 1818; repr. 1828 and 1830 [for details, see Mendes, p. 306]).

Andrea de Nerciat, *Félicia ou Mes fredaines* (1775).

——, *La Matinée libertine ou Les Moments bien employés* (1787).

——, *Le Doctorat impromptu* (1788); (translated as *The Unexpected Love-Lesson*, by D. Leslie, London, 1970).

——, *Monrose ou Le Libertin Par fatalité* (1792).

——, *Mon Noviciat ou Les Joies de Lolote* (1792); (translated as *The Pleasures of Lolotte*, by Frank Pomeranz, introduction by J.-P. Spencer, London: W. H. Allen, 1987).

——, *Les Anaphrodites* (1793).

Rétif de la Bretonne, *L'Anti-Justine* (1797).

Notes

PREFACE

1   For all its faults, such as the absence of any precise definitions, or any serious attempt to analyse the literature, and even though it consists largely of summaries in a rather irritating style, the main work on this subject is still Sarane Alexandrian's *Histoire de la littérature érotique* (Paris: Seghers, 1989).

2   Some of these issues are considered, but are not central to the present essay.

3   A key text on the effects of pornographic literature is that of the preacher Massillon (1663–1742), *Discours inédit sur le danger des mauvaises lectures* (published in 1817). This work was written as a reply to defences of the erotic novel: 'If people were as insensitive to this literature as you seem to suppose, then why all these movements and struggles, this troubling of the mind, and all the emotions that are all too apparent and which you cannot conceal after reading such lascivious works?' (p. 11).

4   See Claude Labrosse, *Lire au XVIIIe siècle: la Nouvelle Héloïse et ses lecteurs* (Lyons, Presses Universitaires de Lyons, 1985).

5   Anne Vincent-Buffault, *Histoire des larmes: XVIe–XVIIIe siècles* (Marseilles, Rivages, 1986). For the English translation, see *The History of Tears: Sensibility and Sentimentality in France*, trans. Teresa Briggeman (London: Macmillan, 1991).

6   Jean-Jacques Rousseau, *Confessions*, book I, p. 40 in the Pléiade edition. For the English translation, see *Confessions*, ed. P. N. Furbank (London: David Campbell, 1992), p. 34.

7   According to Pascal Pia's *Les Livres de l'Enfer du XVIe siecle à nos*

jours, 2 vols (Paris, 1978); editions of *L'Histoire de Dom Bougre, Portier des Chartreux*, were published in 1924, 1960 and 1969 and editions of *Thérèse philosophe* in 1910 and 1961.

8 Etienne Souriau, *Les 200,000 situations dramatiques* (Paris, 1950).

INTRODUCTION: 'LES MOTS ET LES CHOSES'

1 See Pierre Guiraud, *Dictionnaire historique, stylistique, étymologique de la littérature érotique, précédé d'une introduction sur les structures étymologiques du vocabulaire érotique* (Paris, 1978).

2 'Faire cattleya' *A la recherche du temps perdu*, ed. P. Clarac and A. Ferré, Bibliothèque de la Pléiade, 3 vols (Paris, 1954), II, p. 28. 'Cattleya' is derived from the name of William Cattley, a patron of botany in the nineteenth century, and is used to designate a type of orchid found in Central America and Brazil. The plant produces heavy and handsome violet, rose or yellow flowers, and is apparently the only orchid to have a scent (*OED*, II, p. 995, and *Robert Dictionnaire de la langue française*, II, p. 407).

3 Sylvain Maréchal, *Contes saugrenus* (Paris, Bibliothèque des curieux, 1927).

4 Salvador Dali, *Le Mythe tragique de l'Angélus de Millet (interprétation paranoïaque)*, 2nd edn (Paris, 1978).

5 Rétif de la Bretonne, *Le Pornographe, ou idées d'un honnête homme*, preface by Béatrice Didier (Paris, 1977).

6 Lamoignon de Malesherbes, *Mémoires sur la librairie et sur la liberté de presse* (Paris: Pillet, 1814).

7 Henri Martin and Roger Chartier, *Histoire de l'édition française*, 2: *Le Livre triomphant* (Paris, 1984), sections 1.2.2 and 1.3.2.

CHAPTER 1 THE IMPORTANCE OF EROTIC LITERATURE IN THE EIGHTEENTH CENTURY

1 Pietro Aretino, born in Arezzo (1492–1556), was the author of satirical portraits along with sundry erotica. For a biography, see James Cleugh, *The Divine Aretino: Pietro of Arezzo, 1492–1556: a Biography* (London, 1965).

2 Jean M. Goulemot, 'Démons, merveilles et philosophie à l'Âge

classique', in *Annales: Economies, Sociétés, Civilisations*, 35, 6 (1980), 1223–50.

3 On these works, see *L'Enfer de la Bibliothèque nationale* (Paris: Fayard, 1988), vol. 7 ('Oeuvres érotiques du XVIIe siècle').

4 The expression is used by Sarane Alexandrian (*Histoire de la littérature érotique*), and reveals a strain of thought common to both those who praised erotic literature and those who condemned it. It can be found in Louis Pierre Manuel's *La Bastille dévoilée* (1789) as well as in Michelet's account of the Ancien Régime, and of course in the works of the Goncourt brothers (*L'Amour au XVIIIe siècle*, Paris, 1875).

5 For documents, see F. Funck Brentano, *Les Lettres de cachet, 1659– 1789* (Paris: Imprimerie nationale, 1903), and F. Ravaison Mollien, *Les Archives de la Bastille, 1866–1904*, 19 vols (esp. vols 15–19).

6 See Henri and Chartier, *Histoire de l'édition française*, 2, pp. 76– 83 ('La Censure') and 2, pp. 84–91 ('La Police du livre'); also N. Hermann Mascard, *La Censure des livres à Paris, 1750–1789* (Paris, 1968), and J.-P. Belin, *Le Commerce des livres prohibés à Paris de 1750 à 1789* (Paris, 1913).

7 Funck Brentano (*Les Lettres de cachet*) argues that there was a shift towards the arrest of *convulsionnaires* in the 1760s.

8 Diderot, *Mémoire sur la liberté de presse*, ed. Jacques Proust (Paris, 1963).

9 Cited in Hermann Mascard, *La Censure des livres*, p. 22.

10 D'Hémery kept a diary of the Book Trade from 1750 to 1769 and a list of booksellers and authors during the 1750s.

11 Hermann Mascard, *La Censure des livres*, p. 22.

12 Hermann Mascard, *La Censure des livres*, p. 45.

13 Belin, *Le Commerce des livres prohibés*, p. 43.

14 Robert Darnton's work is an essential contribution to the diffusion of underground literature. For some of his more general studies of the book-trade at this period, see *The Business of the Enlightenment: a Publishing History of the 'Encyclopédie', 1775–1800* (London: Belknap Press, 1979), *The Literary Underground of the Old Regime* (London: Harvard University Press, 1982), *Revolution in Print: the Press in France, 1775–1800* (Berkeley: University of California Press/New York Public Library, 1989) and, more specifically related to the trade in obscene publications, 'Trade in the taboo: the life of a clandestine book dealer in provincial France', in *The Widening Cricle: Essays on the Circulation of Literature in*

Eighteenth-Century Europe, ed. P. J. Korshin (Philadelphia: Philadelphia University Press, 1976), pp. 11–83.

15 Belin, *Le Commerce des livres prohibés*, pp. 103–4.

16 L. S. Mercier, *Le Tableau de Paris* (Amsterdam, 1782–3), 5, pp. 61–4.

17 Funck Brentano (*Les Lettres de cachet*), entries for the year 1749, esp. numbers 4074, 4081, 4083, 4084 and so on.

18 Funck Brentano (*Les Lettres de cachet*), entry for the year 1749, number 4074.

19 Robert Darnton has analysed several cases in his article 'Trade in the taboo: the life of a clandestine book dealer in provincial France'.

20 See Funck Brentano (*Les Lettres de cachet*), entries for the year 1749.

21 See Chantal Thomas, *La Reine scélérate, Marie Antoinette dans les pamphlets* (Paris, 1989), and also the catalogue from the exhibition *Revolution in Print: the Press in France, 1775–1800* (London and Berkeley, 1989) and Jean-Jacques Pauvert, *Estampes érotiques révolutionnaires: la Révolution française et l'obscenité* (Paris, 1989).

22 Claude [François, Xavier] Mercier, known as Mercier de Compiègne because he was born in there in 1763, is a prime example of a man who took up pornography out of necessity. Pierre-Jean-Baptiste Nougaret (1742–1823) is the epitome of the mediocre compiler. He tried his hand at a variety of genres with varying success. Fighting alongside Voltaire in the philosophical battles of the time, he did not neglect the writing of erotic works either. In 1769 he published *La Capucinade, histoire sans vraisemblance*, for which he was imprisoned in the Bastille. This work was reprinted in 1797 under the title of *Aventures galantes de Jérôme, frère capucin*. He then went on to pen *Ainsi va le monde* in 1769, which was reprinted in 1797, 1799 and 1801 under the title of *Les Jolis Péchés d'une marchande de modes ou Ainsi va le monde*. The bibliography of his works is lengthy. A precise analysis would show that he was quite capable of playing on the fashionable titles of the day, whether they were pornographic or not. Thus, he published *Le Tableau mouvant de Paris* on the model of L. S. Mercier's *Le Tableau de Paris* (1786), and then *L'Ancien et le nouveau Paris* (1798). His novel *Le Danger des circonstances ou Les Nouvelles liaisons dangereuses* attempted to take advantage of the success of Laclos' work. He also published *La Paysanne pervertie ou Les Moeurs des grandes villes* (1777), following in the footsteps of Rétif de la Bretonne.

23 Diderot, *Le Neveu de Rameau*, in *Oeuvres*, ed. André Billy, Bibliothèque de la Pléiade (Paris: Gallimard, 1951), pp. 395–474, here pp. 426–7. For the English translation, see *Rameau's Nephew*, trans. Jacques Barzan, 2nd edn (London: Encyclopedia Britannica, 1990), p. 274.

24 Rousseau, *Confessions*, ed. P. N. Furbank (London: David Campbell, 1992), p. 34.

25 Diderot, *Jacques le Fataliste*, in *Oeuvres*, pp. 475–711. For the English translation, see *Jacques the Fatalist*, trans. Martin Henry (Harmondsworth: Penguin, 1986), p. 181.

26 *Jacques the Fatalist*, p. 166.

CHAPTER 2 THE EFFECTS OF READING EROTIC LITERATURE

1 Tissot's *L'Onanisme, dissertation sur les maladies produites par la masturbation*, dates from 1760. The most recent Modern French edition is that of Théodore Tarczylo (Paris: Le Sycomore, 1980). Bienville's *La Nymphomanie ou Traité de la fureur utérine* was published in 1771 (ed. Jean-Marie Goulemot, Paris: Le Sycomore, 1980). For English translations, see *Onanism by S. A. Tissot and Nymphomania by D. T. Bienville*, ed. Randolph Trumbach, Marriage, Sex and the Family in England, 1660–1800, vol. 13 (London: Garland, 1985).

2 Rousseau, *Confessions*, book 1 (p. 40 in the Pléiade edition), p. 34 in the English translation.

3 Nicolas Edme Rétif de la Bretonne, *Monsieur Nicolas ou Le Coeur humain dévoilé*, ed. Pierre Testud (Paris: Bibliothèque de la Pléiade, 1990), pp. 1042–4. English translation after *Monsieur Nicolas or The Human Heart Laid Bare*, trans. and ed. Robert Baldick (London: Barrie & Rockliff, 1966), pp. 341–3.

4 Bienville, *Nymphomanie*, p. 111.

5 Bienville, *Nymphomanie*, p. 124.

6 Bienville, *Nymphomanie*, p. 73.

7 Rétif de la Bretonne, *Monsieur Nicolas*, p. 930 (p. 316 in the English translation).

8 *Jacques le Fataliste*, pp. 653–4 for the French text, pp. 197–8 in the English translation.

9 *Jacques le Fataliste*, pp. 652–3 for the French text, pp. 196–7 in the English translation.

10 *Jacques le Fataliste*, p. 652 for the French text, p. 197 in the English translation.
11 *Jacques le Fataliste*, p. 648 for the French text, p. 192 in the English translation.
12 *Jacques le Fataliste*, p. 642 for the French text, p. 187 in the English translation.
13 *Jacques le Fataliste*, p. 684 for the French text, p. 227 in the English translation.
14 *Jacques le Fataliste*, p. 705 for the French text, p. 248 in the English translation.
15 *Jacques le Fataliste*, p. 710 for the French text, p. 253 in the English translation.
16 *Jacques le Fataliste*, p. 710 for the French text, p. 253 in the English translation.
17 See *Les Bijoux indiscrets*, chapter 7.
18 *Jacques le Fataliste*, p. 477 for the French text, p. 23 in the English translation.
19 *Jacques le Fataliste*, p. 478 for the French text, p. 24 in the English translation.
20 *Jacques le Fataliste*, pp. 633–4 for the French text, pp. 176–7 in the English translation.
21 Compare this with the account given in Michael Fried's *Absorption and Theatricality: Painting and Beholder in the Age of Diderot* (London: University of California Press, 1980).

CHAPTER 3 THE POWERS OF THE LITERARY IMAGINATION

1 It is only in the original manuscript of *Les Infortunes de la vertu*, not published until in the early part of this century by Guillaume Apollinaire, that Justine retains the pseudonym Sophie (on the textual tradition of the work, see *Justine or the Misfortunes of Virtue*, ed. and trans. Alan Hall Water (London: Neville Spearman, 1964), introduction, p. 51).
2 Sade, *Misfortunes of Virtue*, p. 69.
3 This analysis owes much to the as yet unpublished work of Didier Masseau on the evolution of narrative forms and the status of the novel at the end of the eighteenth century.
4 Marquis of Feuquières, *Phantasiologie ou Lettres philosophiques à Madame de ... sur la faculté imaginative*, letter 1, p. 26.
5 Marquis of Feuquières, *Phantasiologie*, letter 3, p. 88.

6 Baron of Holbach, *Les Plaisirs de l'imagination, poème en trois chants par M. Akenside, traduit de l'anglais par le Baron d'Holbach* (Amsterdam, 1759), p. 8.

7 Helvetius, *De l'homme* (London, 1773), 2, p. 186.

8 See Labrosse, *Lire au XVIIIe siècle, La Nouvelle Héloïse et ses lecteurs.*

9 Louis-Sebastien Mercier, *Mon bonnet de nuit* (Lausanne, 1785), 1, p. 197.

10 See the accounts of Tissot and Bienville in chapter 2.

11 Especially those of Madame de Miremont, *Traité de l'éducation des femmes et cours complet d'instruction*, 7 vols (Paris, 1779).

12 Rousseau, *Emile or on Education*, trans. Allan Bloom (Harmondsworth: Penguin, 1991), p. 321. For the French text, see *Oeuvres complètes*, Bibliothèque de la Pléiade (Paris: Gallimard, 1954), 4, p. 645.

13 Quoted by Labrosse, *Lire au XVIIIe siècle, La Nouvelle Héloïse et ses lecteurs.*

CHAPTER 4 THE LIMITS OF PORNOGRAPHIC WRITING

1 See the works of Jean Duprun on Sade's borrowings from contemporary philosophical writers. A synthesis can be found in the introduction to the Pléiade edition of his works (Paris, 1990).

2 On the publication of *Ma conversion ou Le Libertin de qualité*, see *L'Enfer de la Bibliothèque nationale*, 1.

3 *Ma conversion*, p. 38.

4 *Ma conversion*, p. 70.

5 *Ma conversion*, p. 121.

6 *Ma conversion*, p. 67.

7 *Ma conversion*, p. 104.

8 *Ma conversion*, p. 80.

9 *Ma conversion*, p. 82.

10 Racine, *Phèdre*, Act V, scene vi.

11 Corneille, *Le Cid*, Act III, scene iv.

12 *Ma conversion*, pp. 71–2.

13 *Ma conversion*, p. 96.

14 *Ma conversion*, p. 58.

15 *Ma conversion*, p. 102.

16 *Ma conversion*, p. 54.

17 *Ma conversion*, p. 63.

CHAPTER 5　CLANDESTINE LITERATURE AND
THE ART OF SELF-DESIGNATION

1　'Mars, ô Vénus te devait ses loisirs'.
2　The citation appears to have been invented. There is no equivalent line in Petronius' *Satyricon*.
3　The quotations are drawn from Virgil's *Aeneid*, Phaedrus' *Fables*, Persius' *Satires*, Ovid's *Amores*, Lucretius' *De Rerum Naturae*, the poetry of Catullus and Martial's *Epigrams*. While the range is quite broad, it does not exceed what might have been the learning of a man of reasonable standing in the eighteenth century. None of the quotations are actually obscene, even those from Catullus or Martial. The references simply serve to provide some cultural legitimacy for erotic literature.
4　See, for example, *L'Art priapique, parodie des deux premiers chants de l'Art poétique par un octogénaire*: 'I have lived and I would like to be of use to those who have lived' (Duclos, *Considérations sur les moeurs*). 'At the sign of Gulled Boileau ['Boileau dindonné']' (1764).
5　*Les Monuments du culte secret des Dames romaines* (1787).
6　*Les Lettres galantes et philosophiques de deux nonnes, publiées par un apôtre du libertinage* (1777).
7　*Les Lauriers ecclésiastiques ou Campagnes de l'abbé de T . . .* (1748).
8　*Histoire merveilleuse et édifiante de Godemiché, trouvée dans un ancien manuscrit de la Bibliothèque de la sacrée congrégation des nonnes, Par l'abbé D . . . , à Rome* (1776).
9　*Le Cabinet de Lampsaque . . .* (1784).
10　*Le Bordel national . . .* (1790).
11　*Les Reclusières de Vénus* (1750).
12　*Anandria, ou Les Confessions de mademoiselle Sapho* (1789).
13　*Le Bordel national . . .* (1790).
14　*Les Rendez-vous de Madame Elisabeth . . .* (1790)
15　*Les Lauriers ecclésiastiques . . .* (1748).
16　*Histoire de Dom B . . .* 'Philotanus' means 'Love of the anus'.
17　*Le Petit-neveu de l'Arétin . . .* (1800).
18　*Les Amours, galanterie ou Passe-temps des actrices . . .* (1800). 'Couillopolis': pun on *couilles*, 'balls'.
19　*Les Coutumes théâtrales ou Scènes secrètes des foyers . . .* (1793). 'Foutropolis': pun on *foutre*, 'to fuck'.
20　*Les Derniers Soupirs de la garce en pleurs . . .* (L'An second de la

bienheureuse fouterie (i.e., 1790)). 'Branlinos': pun on *branler*, 'to masturbate', 'to wank'.

21 *Les Petits Bougres au manège* ... (L'An second de la liberté (i.e., 1790)). 'Enculons': pun on *enculer*, 'to sodomise'.

22 *Requête et décret en faveur des putains* ... (L'An second de la régénération foutative (i.e., 1790)). 'Gamahuchons': pun on *gamahucher*, 'to have anal intercourse with'.

23 *Les Coutumes théâtrales ou Scènes secrètes des foyers.*

24 *Les Derniers Soupirs de la garce en pleurs.*

25 *La Nouvelle Messeline, tragédie* (1774).

26 *Dom Bougre aux Etats Généraux.*

27 'Sur l'imprimerie à Démocratis, aux dépens des fouteurs démagogues, 1792'.

28 'A Gamahuchon [pun on *gamahucher*, 'to have anal intercourse with'], et se trouve chez toutes les Fouteries nationales, l'An II de la régénération foutative'.

29 *Les Derniers Soupirs de la garce en pleurs.* 'L'An I de la bienheureuse fouterie'.

30 *Les Petits Bougres au manège.*

31 'Alphonse, dit l'impuissant ... A Origénie, chez Jean qui ne peut, au grand eunuque, 1740'.

32 'A Namur, à l'enseigne de Boileau dindonné'.

33 'Chez feue la Veuve Girouard très-connue où l'adjectif est à prendre au sens biblique et affligée parfois d'une coupure (con-nue) qui lui donne tout son sens érotique'.

CHAPTER 6 MEANS TO AN END: THE STRATEGIES
OF EROTIC NARRATIVE

1 Rétif de la Bretonne, *L'Anti-Justine*, in *L'Enfer de la Bibliothèque nationale*, 2 (Paris, 1985), foreword, p. 285.

2 Miguel de Cervantes, *Don Quixote*, trans. P. A. Motteux (London: Everyman, 1991), part 1, book 1, chap. 1, p. 5.

3 Massillon, *Discours inédit*, p. 10.

4 *Jacques le Fataliste*, p. 486 for the French text, p. 32 in the English translation.

5 Gervaise de la Touche, *Histoire de Dom Bougre*, in *L'Enfer de la Bibliothèque nationale*, 3 (Paris, 1985), p. 50.

6 *Histoire de Dom Bougre*, p. 56.

7 Mirabeau, *Le Rideau levé ou L'Education de Laure*, in *L'Enfer de la Bibliothèque nationale*, 1 (Paris, 1984), pp. 323–4.
8 Mirabeau, *Ma conversion*, p. 63.
9 Mirabeau, *Le Rideau levé*, p. 39.
10 Beaumarchais, *Le Mariage de Figaro*, trans. as *Figaro's Marriage* by Jacques Barzun in *Phaedra and Figaro* (New York: Farrar, Strauss & Cudahy, 1961), p. 129.

APPENDIX

1 Mendes, pp. 314–17.

Index